THOMAS HARDY'S
UNIVERSE . .

THOMAS HARDY'S UNIVERSE · A STUDY OF A POET'S MIND *By* ERNEST BRENNECKE, Jr.

HASKELL HOUSE
Publishers of Scholarly Books
NEW YORK
1966

" Unadjusted impressions have their value, and the road to a true philosophy of life seems to lie in humbly recording diverse readings of its phenomena as they are forced upon us by chance and change."

T. H., in Preface to
Poems of the Past and the Present.

FOREWORD

THE ARTISTIC and spiritual descent of the author of *Tess*, *Jude*, and *The Dynasts*, as it has already been frequently traced by critical genealogists presents an imposing maze of relationships and cross-relationships to crowned heads of the world's literary aristocracy. The stern singers of Israel, chanting of love, justice, and retribution,—Æschylus, prophet of a relentless Nemesis, lover of wars, tumults, and polysyllabic ponderosities of language,—the creator of Beowulf, with his ironical humour and his vision of Wessex moors pregnant with the doom of Wyrd,—the heroic Elizabethan tragedians,—the Goethe of Faust's celestial machinery,—the Promethean Shelley,—Voltaire and Leopardi—all these figures have in turn supplied standards, parallels, and "influences" for the judicial critics of Thomas Hardy's novels, lyrics, and dramas.

Indeed, if we consider the boldness of the Hardy-vocabulary, the "packed" versification of his poems, the closely knit structure of his novels, the cosmic surge of *The Dynasts*, the restricted geographical field upon which universal and inevitable human dramas are revealed with a unique courage, sincerity, and flashes of grim earthly humour, we soon discover the impossibility of penetrating to the roots of his artistic organism without invoking the shades of his gigantic æsthetic progenitors.

But when we closely consider Hardy's "philosophy," by which I mean the prevailing colour and composition of the screen through which he views the world in his writings, we find these invocations rather futile. For Hardy is far more conscious of his attitude than any of those æsthetic atavars of his ; each succeeding book gives evidence that throughout his life he has become more and more keenly aware of the far-reaching logical implications of the *Weltanschauung* he assumed from the very first, or rather, of those more sombre harmonies of the human mind at which his art became vocal. A philosopher, in the stricter sense of the word, one might almost say a " professional philosopher," must be summoned to provide a coherent system of thought to place in convincing juxtaposition to the Hardy-system.

" Hardy-system "—Hardy himself would probably object to the term. I recall his insistence, when he gathered, in the course of a casual conversation, that I had an essay of this kind in mind,—his insistence that I could under no consideration ignore his disavowal of the professional philosopher's attitude, as he voiced it in the *Preface* to *The Dynasts*. " Their doctrines," he wrote, referring to the cosmic comments of his celestial spirits, " are but tentative, and are advanced with but little eye to a systematized philosophy warranted to lift ' the burthen of the mystery ' of this unintelligible world."

Neither this consideration, however, nor the undoubted fact that Hardy himself does not, in his life, continually play the satanic chords sounded by his books, need deter his sincerely curious readers from attempting to analyse the totality of the impressions given by his writings (a singularly coherent totality), and from inquiring which logical philosophical structure that totality most closely resembles.

Without criticizing Hardy's philosophy as one would criticize, say, Spinoza's, conceiving it as a system really " warranted to lift the burthen of the mystery," dissecting it, and examining each detail with the bright and merciless instruments of a rigid induction and deduction, one may without great qualms yield to the temptation of observing, broadly, how the " tentative " and " unadjusted " scheme of the greatest living English poet fits in with those of such thinkers, also " vocal to tragedy," who have chosen to eschew imaginative writing and to expose their attitudes more strictly in accordance with the laws of logic.

If, indeed, one may attempt to come to grips with the intellectual content of Hardy (and surely one may !—a more exhilarating mental sport can scarcely be imagined), it is as impossible to succeed in such an attempt without indicating parallelisms from philosophers as it is to discuss his art without pointing out literary parallels. In particular, it is quite impossible, from the first, to ignore Schopenhauer,—and before one has proceeded very far, Schopenhauer is found to have usurped practically the whole discussion.

The form in which the following essay has been cast may therefore seem at first to give the disagreeable *mal-de-mer* effect of a constant and monotonous see-sawing between the English poet and the German philosopher. This perhaps too *echt-deutsch* structure proved, however, to be almost the inevitable form for the study, inasmuch as it was found necessary not only to erect the Hardy-universe out of materials supplied by some thirty heterogeneous volumes, but also to marshal the complementary Schopenhauer-world to a great extent. In my recognition of the fact that Schopenhauer never synthesized his philosophy into a perfectly clear-cut geometrical figure, I count on the sympathetic agreement of many readers of his loosely cast books.

I might add that the " Hardy-universe," as I have developed it in the pages to follow, is based on all his published writings pertinent to my purpose, which have appeared previously to the *Late Lyrics and Earlier*. A chronological list of these will be found in the Appendix. At the moment of writing, the verses of his *Famous Tragedy of the Queen of Cornwall* are being simultaneously rehearsed by the Hardy Players at Dorchester and struck off the presses in Edinburgh.

E. B.

PARIS,
November 24, 1923.

CONTENTS

PAGE

FOREWORD 7

CHAPTER

I. HARDY AND SCHOPENHAUER 13

II. A METAPHYSICAL BIOGRAPHY OF THOMAS HARDY 35

III. "WHAT OF THE IMMANENT WILL?" . . 54

IV. "EARTH'S JACKACLOCKS" 88

V. "UNWEETING WHY OR WHENCE" . . . 109

VI. THE ULTIMATE HOPE 128

APPENDIX—

CHRONOLOGICAL LIST OF HARDY'S WRITINGS . 149

INDEX 151

11

THOMAS HARDY'S UNIVERSE

CHAPTER ONE

HARDY AND SCHOPENHAUER

THAT THOMAS HARDY is not a novelist who tells stories merely for the diversion of his audience, nor a poet who delights merely in the sensuous and suggestive appeal of cleverly built emotional word-structures, is apparent even to the most superficial of his readers. One recognizes, inevitably, that Hardy's underlying aim has always been the conveyance of ideas, and that he has throughout his literary career drawn from the depths of a definite and fairly consistent world-view.

He was really a philosopher, in his own right, long before his mind formed intimate acquaintance with those immortal spirits whose " nocturnal lamp illumines the universe." Long before he acquired philosophical learning he was the possessor of the philosophical temperament which enabled him to approach the commonest phenomenon of life in such a manner as to lay bare its real significance in a general scheme of things, and to present an apparently trivial situation in such a way as to make it the vehicle for the communication of an ultimate truth. In some of his earliest poems, written at a time when he could barely have known the names of the great thinkers of the past, he was constrained to grapple with metaphysical problems that have been burning in the heart of thinking mankind since the dawn of history.

There is ample evidence also that as time went on he took up the study of the philosophical classics, and that he did it with the earnestness which is characteristic of a man whose very nature would not permit him to approach any subject with superficiality. His casual mentioning of philosophers of various schools [1] affords no tangible clue to the interpretation of his general views. Of the greatest importance, however, is the fact that he has adopted and developed with increasing clearness and definiteness a precise philosophical phraseology that leaves little doubt as to the place he occupies in the world of thought.

It seems to be universally recognized at the present time by everybody interested in the subject that there is the closest intellectual affinity between Arthur Schopenhauer and Thomas Hardy. He himself has freely and frequently admitted it.[2] Mr. Edmund Gosse, it is true, in a letter to M. Hedgcock,[3] has

---

[1] Diogenes Lærtius (*A Pair of Blue Eyes*, XXXII) ; Utilitarianism (*The Hand of Ethelberta*, XXXVI) ; Plato's Socrates (*The Return of the Native*, III, iii) ; Spinoza, and Socratic " εἰρώνεια " (*The Woodlanders*, XVI, and *Jude the Obscure*, I, xi) ; Schleiermacher (*The Woodlanders*, XIX) ; Peripatetic School (*The Woodlanders*, XLI) ; *Dictionnaire Philosophique* (*Tess*, XLVI) ; Platonic philosophers (*The Well-Beloved*, Preface) ; and Humboldt (*Jude*, IV, iii).

[2] E.g. in a letter to Dr. Garwood. See Helen Garwood, *Thomas Hardy, an Illustration of the Philosophy of Schopenhauer*, Philadelphia, Winston, 1911, p. 11.

[3] F. A. Hedgcock, *Thomas Hardy, Penseur et Artiste*, Paris, Hachette, 1909, p. 499. It is evident that Mr. Gosse has here missed the real point at issue when he assumes as a matter of course that Hardy's philosophy can be summed up in the word " pessimism." This is the usual fatal error of the Hardy-critic.

denied the possibility that Schopenhauer exercised any influence on Hardy's work before 1874 ; and it is perfectly believable that the broad outlines of his philosophy, and the rather vague and less sharply defined terms in which he had presented it up to that time, were developed in complete independence of the writings of Schopenhauer. But it is equally apparent that in his later works a definite and unmistakable Schopenhauerian phraseology is adopted, and that the " Overworld " scenes of *The Dynasts* could not possibly have been composed if Schopenhauer had not previously written *Die Welt als Wille und Vorstellung*.

Hardy's dependence upon Schopenhauer presents itself as a problem which can find its adequate answer only in a detailed comparison of their ideas, and need not be discussed at present ; but another, and a more important question arises—the question as to the nature and the extent of the philosophical parallelism between the two writers. Do we class them together simply because they are pessimists and look at life through dark or distorted lenses ? The general recognition of the value of Schopenhauer's philosophy was retarded chiefly by the unfortunate circumstance that immediately after the appearance of his principal work he was classified and tabulated—and pigeonholed—by the philosophical fraternity and in philosophical journals as a pessimist ; and it was not until shortly before his death that scholars became aware that he was not simply a pessimist, but a pessimist who had developed his philosophical system from the fundamental conception of the Will as the Thing-in-itself. Pessimism is only a small and by no means the most important section of the philosophy of Schopenhauer. It is only one of the practical results of his fundamental conceptions, and even as such it is not his final word. For his pessimism is very far removed indeed from that general undefined attitude of mental gloominess that "always looks on the dark side of things," or, as Dr. Garwood picturesquely expresses it, "sees only the hole, and not the doughnut." [1] And while his reader may at first be struck, and perhaps repelled, by the extreme violence with which the general worthlessness of life is exposed, he will eventually detect a decided gleam of hope, one that points forward to a better eventuality than eternal misery.

It appears therefore as an entirely unwarranted limitation of the subject to confine the study of the mental parallelism between Hardy and Schopenhauer, as is usually done,[2] to the one feature of " pessimism." If Hardy were merely to be classified as a pessimist, why not compare him with other pessimists—why not, for instance, look for the roots of his world-view in the ancient Hindu-philosophy ? For pessimism is as old as the world, and there were many pessimists before Schopenhauer. The spiritual affinity between the two writers becomes apparent and convincing only when it is observed that Hardy, like Schopenhauer, bases his views on the fundamental conception of the Will, which he makes the foundation for all his thoughts.

While, then, the place of both writers in the world of thought, as well as the significance of their message, is determined by the fact that both are prophets of the Immanent Will, it should be observed that their respective methods may be very different, and that little outward similarity may obtain between the

[1] Helen Garwood, *Hardy*, p. 16.
[2] For instance, by Garwood, and Hedgcock, in the few pages he devotes to the subject.

garb in which they clothe their ideas. For Schopenhauer, although keenly appreciative of the beautiful in all the arts and endowed with exceptional literary talents, is nevertheless a philosopher first ; and Hardy, although he has acquired an intimate acquaintance with the problems of philosophy during a long life devoted to accurate observation and careful meditation, is primarily a poet. Therefore, while both deal with life and strive to explain it, each one chooses a method of approach peculiar to the chief interests of his own life. The philosopher's domain is *abstract thought as primarily independent from* spatial and temporal manifestations ; the poet's domain is *concrete truth as underlying* spatial and temporal manifestations. The philosopher's usual way of reasoning is to find and state a principle and to evolve from it synthetically a system of ideas ; the poet's intellectual process is the reverse ; to observe and to describe a concrete condition as the final result of a chain of causes and to resolve it analytically in order to find the underlying principle. It is not an unreasonable procedure, then, to try and detect the same fundamental concepts in both Hardy and Schopenhauer, even when they seem to employ divergent processes of thought and different languages for the final expression of these concepts.

The starting-point of Schopenhauer's philosophy is the Kantian principle that man has no objective knowledge of the real nature of the empirical world, but that it is present in his mind only as a phenomenon of consciousness, determined and limited by the necessary forms of all intellectual processes : time, space, and causality. The recognition of the fact that " the world is my idea," produces in him who really comprehends it something akin to an operation for optical cataract, and brings about in the mind of him who has fully grasped it a fundamental change comparable to a spiritual regeneration. He is aware, henceforth, that what he knows is not the sun and the earth, but only the eye that sees the sun, and the hand that touches the earth.[1]

Hardy's first step in the direction of the idealistic viewpoint may be discovered in those passages in which he expresses his deep-seated longing to escape from the world of fact and experience. One of his very first poems begins : " In Vision I Roamed the Flashing Firmament." [2] Oppressed by the irksome sense of the limitations of time and space, the thought of the young poet ventures into the vast and unknown depths of the Universe and, " in footless traverse through ghast heights of sky," presses on " to the last chambers of the Monstrous Dome." Having taken his standpoint in Infinity all distances vanish and " any spot on our own Earth seems Home." The sick grief that the beloved one is far away gives way to pleasant thankfulness in the realization that all separating barriers are removed and nothing is far from the mind that lives in Infinity. In one of the earliest prose-works, *A Pair of Blue Eyes*,[3] Knight muses—

Such occasions as these seem to compel us to roam outside ourselves, far away from the fragile frame we live in, and to expand till our perception grows so vast that our physical reality bears no sort of proportion to it.

Similar expressions are found scattered throughout Hardy's works. In one of the last lyrics, *For Life*

[1] Schopenhauer, *Die Welt als Wille und Vorstellung*, (hereafter abbreviated Sch. i and ii), vol. i, pp. 33-65 ; vol. ii, pp. 224-7 ; *Parerga und Parà-lipomena*, pp. 15-33 (*Gechichte der Lehre vom Idealen und Realen*).
[2] 1866, in *Wessex Poems* (hereafter abbreviated *WP*).
[3] Chap. xxvii.

Hardy and Schopenhauer

I Had Never Cared Greatly,[1] we may discover the same poetical idealism which fifty years before had inspired some of the early sonnets. Again, as he looks back upon a life full of sincere thought and effort courageously devoted to the realization of unselfish ambitions, he raises his gaze from the sordid life that he touches and feels and sees around him, and contemplates the higher " Life," that

> . . . lifting its hand
> . . . uncloaked a star,
> Uncloaked it from fog-damps afar,
> And showed its beams burning from pole to horizon
> As bright as a brand.
>
> And so, the rough highway forgetting,
> I pace hill and dale
> Regarding the sky,
> Regarding the vision on high,
> And so reillumined have no humour for letting
> My pilgrimage fail.

A still nearer approach to the idealistic viewpoint is to be discovered in two truly remarkable short stories that express Hardy's belief in the supremacy of the mind over bodily conditions. In *The Withered Arm,*[2] he reports a local legend which to his mind demonstrates beyond all doubt that the mind is both the creative principle underlying all visible phenomena and the organizing source of physical existence. A woman's hatred for her successful rival is so strong that when she, in her imagination, grasps the arm of her enemy, the undeniable mark of her fingers appears on the arm of the actual person, and causes paralysis of the limb. The story is told with a verisimilitude in detail that denotes both consummate

[1] 1917, in *Moments of Vision* (hereafter abbreviated *MV*).
[2] 1888, in *Wessex Tales.*

artistry, and at the least, a real sympathy on the part of the author with the tale he recounts. That it is perhaps even more than mere sympathy seems to be the import of these remarks in the Preface—[1]

Since writing this story some years ago I have been reminded by an aged friend who knew ". Rhoda Brook " that, in relating her dream, my forgetfulness has weakened the facts out of which the tale grew. In reality it was while lying down on a hot afternoon that the incubus oppressed her and she flung it off, with the results upon the body of the original as described. To my mind the occurrence of such a vision in the daytime is more impressive than if it had happened in a midnight dream. Readers are therefore asked to correct the misrelation, which affords an instance of how our imperfect memories insensibly formalize the fresh originality of living fact—from whose shape they slowly depart as machine-made castings depart by degrees from the sharp hand-work of the mould.

The same view underlies the second story, *An Imaginative Woman*.[2] The chief character of this tale, a woman, unhappily married, broods with un-abated intensity over the photograph and the mental and physical characteristics of her ideal, the poet Trewe, who, however, commits suicide before she ever manages to see him. After her death, a year later, her unimaginative husband discovers that his and her child bears unmistakable resemblance to the dead poet. Of this story Hardy writes in the Preface—

It turns upon a physical possibility that may attach to women of imaginative temperament, and that is well sup-ported by the experiences of medical men and other observers of such manifestations.[3]

[1] Edition of 1896.
[2] 1893, in *Wessex Tales*.
[3] The same idea underlies Goethe's *Wahlverwandschaften*.

Hardy and Schopenhauer

It should be observed that these expressions of poetical idealism and of belief in the influence of mental action upon physical processes are not idealism in the philosophical sense of the term, but mark only an approach to it. Genuine metaphysical idealism, however, is to be found in many places in the writings of Hardy. There is an abundance of evidence that in the late " eighties " he came under the powerful sway of that line of great thinkers whose first and most illustrious name is that of Plato, whose first representative in modern times is Berkeley, and whose viewpoint is later championed and developed by Kant, Fichte, Hegel, and Schopenhauer. In *The Woodlanders* [1] Fitzpiers, the physician, is made the vehicle of most of the author's patent transcendentalism. We are told that the Doctor is not a practical man, but prefers the ideal world to the real, and that he reads constantly in the works of German metaphysicians.[2] The following sentiments are put into the mouth of the learned physician—

" . . . The design is for once carried out. Nature has at last recovered her lost union with the idea. My thoughts ran in that direction because I had been reading the work of a transcendental philosopher last night, and I dare say it was the dose of Idealism that I received from it that made me scarcely able to distinguish between reality and fancy." [3]

" . . . Strangeness is not in the nature of a thing—but in its relation to something extrinsic. . . . " [4]

" . . . Human love is a subjective thing—the essence itself of man, as the great thinker Spinoza the philosopher says—*ipsa hominis essentia*—it is joy accompanied by an idea which we project against any suitable object in the line of our vision, just as the rainbow iris is projected against an oak, ash, or elm tree indifferently." [5]

[1] 1887.   [2] Chap. xvi.   [3] Chap. xviii.   [4] Chap. xviii.
[5] Chap. xvi. Note also : " ' Ah, Grammer,' he said, at another time, ' let me tell you the Everything is Nothing. There's only Me and not-Me in the whole world ' " (chap. vi).

Hardy himself has warned his readers against attributing to a writer the philosophy discovered within the inverted commas of the dialogue in his imaginative work,[1] but that Fitzpiers's idealism represents something more than Hardy's effort to introduce an exotic character into his peaceful Wessex countryside, is shown by these selections from the author's own personal remarks to the reader—

Nay, from the highest point of view, to precisely describe a human being, the focus of a universe—how impossible ! But apart from transcendentalism. . . .[2]

He dreamed and mused till his consciousness seemed to occupy the whole space of the woodland around, so little was there of jarring sight or sound to hinder perfect unity with the sentiment of the place.[3]

From now on Hardy is an ardent apostle of idealism, in the philosopher's as well as in the poet's sense of the term. In *Tess of the D'Urbervilles* the transcendental philosophy that was first expressed through the words of Fitzpiers is applied to the conception of the character of the heroine, to whom

Natural processes seemed a part of her own story. Rather they became a part of it, for the world is only a cerebral phenomenon, by all account, and what they seemed they were.[4]

He also says of her that

Troubles and other realities took on themselves a metaphysical impalpability, sinking to mere cerebral phenomena

---

[1] *The Profitable Reading of Fiction* (*Forum*, N.Y., March 1888) : " A philosophy which appears between the inverted commas of a dialogue may, with propriety, be as full of holes as a sieve, if the person or persons who advance it gain any reality of humanity thereby."
[2] Chap. v.   [3] Chap. xix.   [4] Chap. xii.

for quiet contemplation, in place of standing as pressing concretions which chafe body and soul.[1]

and

Upon her sensations, the whole world depended to Tess ; through her existence all her fellow-creatures existed, to her. The very universe itself only came into being for Tess on the particular day in the particular year in which she was born.[2]

Of the traces of idealism in *Jude*, only one need be cited, as it hints at the conception of love around which the whole fabric of *The Well-Beloved* is woven. As the baseness of the character of the woman who has enticed him away from his studies gradually dawns upon the hapless hero, he consoles himself by keeping up

a factitious belief in her. His idea of her was the thing of most consequence, not Arabella herself, he said laconically.[3]

The Well-Beloved, Hardy's last novel, is nothing but a clever application of the Platonic and Shelleyan [4] types of idealism to a rather whimsical story of the successive disappointments in love of a man of whose character he tells us (in the Preface)

Others may see (it) only as one that gave objective continuity and a name to a delicate dream which in a vaguer

[1] Chap. iii.

[2] Chap. xxiii. Note her own expression of her instinctive idealism : " I know that our souls can be made to go outside our bodies when we are alive . . . a very easy way to feel 'em go is to lie on the grass at night and look straight up at some big bright star ; and, by fixing your mind upon it, you will soon find that you are hundreds and hundreds o' miles away from your body, which you don't seem to want at all " (chap. xvi). Cf. Sch. i, p. 185. " Mein Bewusstsein ist der Träger der Welt . . . Daher könnte man auch behaupten, dass wenn, *per impossibile*, ein einziges Wesen, und wäre es das geringste, gänzlich vernichtet wuerde, mit ihm die ganze Welt untergehen muesste."

[3] Part I, chap. viii.

[4] The " motto " for the book is Shelley's " One shape of many names."

form is more or less common to all men, and is by no means new to Platonic philosophers.

We are not surprised, then, when we encounter the clearest expressions of the transcendental train of thought in the later lyrical poems. In *On a Fine Morning*,[1] for instance, conventional religion is treated not as a part of reality but rather as an escape from it. Likewise in *The Dream-Follower* [2] the reader is made acutely aware of the vast gulf that divides the ideal from the real universe. And so it is possible to run through all of the poems, even to the last volume, and continually discover new evidence that Hardy gives unreserved assent to the first fundamental conception of Schopenhauer : " Die Welt ist meine Vorstellung."

But what is this empirical world besides my idea ? What is the significance of this idea ? [3] Is this world merely idea,—in which case it would pass by us like an empty dream and a baseless vision, not worthy of our notice,—or is it something more than idea, and if so, what ? With this question Schopenhauer departs from Kant, and definitely advances beyond him. For while Kant denied the possibility of knowing the real essence of things, and thereby paved the way to scepticism and the intellectual monstrosities of the ultra-idealistic school of Fichte, Schopenhauer pursues the saner method of trying to harmonize the postulates of pure reason with the demands of the immediate human consciousness, and emphatically asserts the knowability of the thing-in-itself.[4] Ideality is not synonymous with unreality. But the endeavours of other philosophers, so Schopenhauer argues, were bound to come to naught, because in their search for

[1] 1899, in *Poems of the Past and the Present* (hereafter abbreviated *PP*).
[2] 1901, *PP*.   [3] Sch. i, 149.   [4] Sch. ii, 221 sqq.

the thing-in-itself they committed the fundamental
error of assuming that " the world as it is in itself "
could be construed from " the world as it appears "
by the application of the principle of sufficient reason.
For while this law holds undisputed sway over the
objective world, furnishing the nexus between its
phenomena and linking them together in an unbroken
chain of necessity, it is not, as Leibnitz and all
Scholastic philosophers assumed, a *veritas æterna* ;
that is to say : it does not possess an unconditioned
validity before, outside of, and above the world, but
it is valid only in the sphere of phenomena ; it does
not extend beyond it, and whatever goal it may lead
to, this goal will prove upon examination to be also
a mere phenomenon and not the thing-in-itself.[1]   It
is futile, therefore, to regard the world as it appears
as the effect of the world as it is in itself, and then,
under the supposition that nothing can be in the
effect which was not contained in the cause, to con-
strue the Non-Ego from the Ego, just as a spider
spins its web out of itself.[2]   No, " nicht von aussen
ist dem Ding an sich beizukommen."[3]

The real nature of the world is indeed like a
citadel into which we never could have gained access
had we not luckily discovered an underground passage
through which we are enabled to press on, as it were
by trickery, to the great mystery. This only key
for the knowledge of the thing-in-itself is the recognition of our bodies as manifestations of will. For
among all phenomena the body alone is given in two
entirely different ways to the investigator, who
becomes an individual only through his identity with
it. It is given to him as an idea in intelligent per-

[1] Sch. i, 70.   [2] Sch., *Vierfache Wurzel,* p. 45 sqq.
[3] Sch. i, 150.

ception, as an object among objects, and as such governed by the laws of objects ; and it is also given to him in an entirely different way as the basis of the thinking subject, and as such is known to him not only indirectly—as everything else—but immediately and directly. Were I merely a subject, it would palpably be impossible for me to know anything about the essence of objects. But I am both, the subject and the object of my thought. Thus in my own personality the chasm made by criticism between the thinking subject and the things in themselves is partly bridged.[1] To wish to know the thing-in-itself in the same manner in which ordinary objects are known, is to wish something contradictory and absurd. By an act of self-consciousness, therefore, the answer to the great question is found by the subject of knowledge, who appears as an individual ; and the answer is : *Will*. This, and this alone, gives him the key to his own existence, reveals to him its significance, shows him the inner mechanism of his being, of his actions, of his movements. Thus the thing-in-itself comes into the consciousness directly and immediately by becoming conscious of itself.[2] Every real and immediate act of will appears immediately as an action on the body. Every action upon the body becomes immediately an action upon the will. It affects the will as pleasure when it is in conformity with it, and it affects it as pain when it is contrary to it. Thus Schopenhauer proclaims the essential identity of body and will. Will is the essential and fundamental thing in man, and his body is nothing but the objectified will, that is, will become idea.[3]

Here, then, we have the key for the understanding

[1] Sch. i, 150 sq. ; ii, 227.   [2] Sch. ii, 227.   [3] Sch. i, 151, 160.

of the world,[1] the " only narrow gate to truth."[2]
For by converting the proposition : I, the subject,
am an object, we are justified in saying : Probably
the object (that is, all the objects, the entire objective
world) is what I am ; its essence is analogous to
mine ; the ultimate principle of the nature of all
other beings is exactly what I find to be the ultimate
principle of my own nature : Will.

It is comparatively easy to see that the bodies of
all animals are peculiarly adapted to their mode of
life, and that Will is in them the organizing principle
and the centre of creative evolution. For their mode
of life does not depend upon the organization of their
bodies, as it may seem at first glance, but quite contrarily, their bodily organization depends upon the
Will manifested in their mode of life. The ox does
not butt because it has horns, but it has horns because
it desired to butt. The bird does not fly because
it has wings, but it has wings because it wanted to
fly.[3] Will is clearly operative in the activity of
animals, but it is blind activity, which is indeed
accompanied by knowledge, but not guided by it.[4]
The house of the snail no less than the house of man
is the product of a Will which objectifies itself in
both phenomena—a Will which works in man according to motives, but in the snail blindly as formative
impulse or instinct.[5]

In the vegetable kingdom Will plays the same part.
Here, too, everything is striving, desire, unconscious
appetition, only here it does not operate according
to motives as in man, nor according to instincts, as

---

[1] Sch. i, 157.
[2] Sch. ii, 227.
[3] Sch., *Der Wille in der Natur*, p. 233 sqq. (*Vergleichende Anatomie*).
[4] Sch. i, 168. " Begleitet, aber nicht geleitet."
[5] Sch. ii, 402 sqq. (*Vom Instinct und Kunsttrieb*).

in animals, but according to stimuli. There is no
essential difference, however, between motive, instinct,
and stimulus, despite the differences in their manifestations. The plant turns to the sun by stimulus, the
animal does likewise, but by instinct, man likewise,
except that here intelligence accompanies the will,
furnishes the motive, and knows what effect the sun
produces on the body.[1]

Only the final step remains to be taken : the
extension of this way of looking at things to those
natural forces acting in accordance with universal and
unchangeable laws, which regulate the movements of
all such bodies as, being without organs, are not
susceptible to stimulus, and having no knowledge,
cannot react on instinct nor respond to motive. But
if we consider attentively even such phenomena of
the inorganic world as are most remote from us—

if we consider the mighty, irresistible urgency with which
the waters hasten to the lowlands, the persistency with which
the magnet always turns to the North Pole, the longing with
which iron flies to the magnet, the eagerness with which the
opposite poles of electricity strive to be reunited, which
tendency, exactly like human desires, is increased by obstacles ;
if we see the crystal quickly and suddenly take form with
such wonderful regularity of construction, which is clearly
only a perfectly definite and accurately determined impulse
in different directions, seized and retained by crystallization ;
if we observe the selective choice with which bodies repel and
attract each other, combine and separate when they are set
free in a fluid state and emancipated from the bonds of rigidity ;
finally, if quite immediately, we feel how a burden, whose
tendency toward the earth has been checked by our body,
continually presses and strains upon it in pursuit of its one
tendency ; if we observe all this, I say, it will require no
great effort of imagination to recognize, even at so great a
distance, our own nature,—the same thing, which in us pursues

[1] Sch. i, 169 sq.

its ends by the light of reason, which in animals responds to instincts, and in plants reacts on stimulus, and which here, in the weakest of its manifestations, strives blindly, dully, one-sidedly, but unchangeably ; which, however, just as the first dim light of dawn must share the name of sunlight with the brightest rays of noon, here as there, can be designated only by the name Will, denoting that which is the real essence of everything in the world, the one kernel of every phenomenon.[1]

If it be urged against this theory that Will is here employed by Schopenhauer in a sense foreign to its common use, the objection cannot be entirely gain-said. But Schopenhauer replies that the thing-in-itself, which never can be object, had, in order to be conceived objectively, to borrow its name from one of its objective manifestations, from the completest of its appearances, the will of man. The designation of the thing-in-itself as Will is therefore a *denominatio a potiori*. The genus is named after its most important species, the direct knowledge of which lies nearer to us and guides us to the indirect knowledge of all other species. But from its narrowest sense as will of man, guided by intelligence and inspired by motive, the idea must be expanded and extended so as to include all possible degrees of semi-conscious and unconscious will and all forms of blind and mute striving in the inorganic world.[2] Nevertheless, Will is the only adequate designation for the thing-in-itself and must not be abandoned for any other term, as, for instance, force. For Will is not the result of force, but, quite contrarily, force is the product and manifestation of Will. The concept of force is an abstraction from the province where cause and effect hold sway, that is, from the objective world of perception. The concept of Will, on the other hand, is of all possible concepts the only one, which has its source not in the phenomenal sphere, but from within, and proceeds from the most immediate consciousness.[1]

If the objection be made that what is here offered as the solution of the great riddle of the universe, is not knowledge in the strict sense of the term, Schopenhauer again readily admits that Will as the thing-in-itself can only be demonstrated, that is, raised from the immediate consciousness, from knowledge in the concrete, to knowledge in the abstract, but it can never be proven, that is, deduced as indirect knowledge from some more direct knowledge, just because it is the most direct knowledge, the philosophical truth κατ᾽ ἐξοχήν.[2] No science can be fully and completely proven, as little as a building can stand in the air : all its proofs must finally rest on perception, that is, on something undemonstrable. Every science arrives in the end at a *qualitas occulta*,[3] and a complete description of nature would only be a catalogue of inexplicable forces.[4]

" My philosophy," Schopenhauer says, " does not presume to explain the ultimate causes of the world. It confines itself to the facts of inner and outer experience, which are accessible to everybody, and points out the true and intimate connection between these facts, without, however, concerning itself with that which may transcend them. It refrains from drawing any conclusions concerning what lies beyond experience. It merely explains the data of sensibility and self-consciousness and strives to understand only the immanent essence of the world." [5]

These words also contain the refutation of the third argument which has sometimes been advanced

[1] Sch. i, 165. [2] Sch. i, 154. " Nachgewiesen," nicht " bewiesen."
[3] Sch. i, 128. [4] Sch. i, 148. [5] Sch. ii, 50.

against Schopenhauer's theory,[1] namely, that Will cannot be the thing-in-itself, as it always presupposes existence. This argument evidently arises from a confounding of " thing-in-itself " with " first cause," a concept which Schopenhauer banishes from the legitimate domain of philosophy. Dogmatic metaphysicians and transcendentalists keep on asking : " why ? " and " whence ? " They forget that " why " means " by what cause," that there are no causes and effects outside of time-succession, and that therefore the " why " and " whence " have no meaning in the sphere of the transcendent to which the forms of time and space cannot be applied.

Will as the thing-in-itself is timeless and spaceless, it can never become object of perception, and is therefore beyond all definition. But Will as the fundamental essence of every phenomenon in the universe reveals its nature in a five-fold form, indicated by five attributes, each of which culminates in a distinct system of thought :

1. The Will is One and Immanent. Therefore there is unity in the world, and the universe must be explained in the terms of Monistic Idealism as opposed to Monistic Materialism and Transcendental Theism.

2. The Will is Groundless and Autonomous. Therefore the universe is ruled by the immutable laws of necessity, determinism is at the base of apparent arbitrariness, and chance is only a form and manifestation of necessity.

3. The Will is Unconscious. Therefore there is absolute superiority of Will over intelligence, and all true psychology must start out from the premise that man is primarily a willing, and not a reasoning being.

---

[1] By Nietzsche, for instance.

4. The Will is Aimless. Therefore Pessimism is the only adequate estimate of life.

5. The Will is Indestructible. Therefore a faint ray of an Ultimate Hope may be discerned.

All this will require further and more detailed exposition.

Meanwhile, let us turn to the first page of Thomas Hardy's great Epic-Drama, *The Dynasts*—

SHADE OF THE EARTH.
What of the Immanent Will and Its designs?

SPIRIT OF THE YEARS.

It works unconsciously, as heretofore,
Eternal artistries in Circumstance,
Whose patterns, wrought by rapt æsthetic rote,
Seem in themselves Its single listless aim,
And not their consequence.

CHORUS OF THE PITIES (aerial music).

Still thus?   Still thus?
Ever unconscious!
An automatic sense
Unweeting why or whence?
Then be the inevitable, as of old,
Although that so it be we dare not hold!

SPIRIT OF THE YEARS.

Hold what you list, fond unbelieving Sprites,
You cannot swerve the pulsion of the Byss,
Which thinking on, yet weighing not Its thought,
Unchecks Its clock-like laws.

SPIRIT SINISTER (aside).

Good, as before,
My little engines, then, will still have play.

SPIRIT OF THE PITIES.

Why doth It so and so, and ever so,
This viewless, voiceless Turner of the Wheel?

Hardy and Schopenhauer

SPIRIT OF THE YEARS.

As one sad story runs, It lends Its heed
To other worlds, being wearied out with this;
Wherefore its mindlessness of earthly woes.
Some, too, havë told at whiles that rightfully
Its warefulness, Its care, this planet lost
When in her early growth and crudity
By bad mad acts of severance men contrived,
Working such nescience by their own device.—
At least, so stands it in some chronicles,
Though not in mine.

SPIRIT OF THE PITIES.

Meet it is, none the less,
To bear in thought that though Its consciousness
May be estranged, engrossed afar, or sealed,
Sublunar shocks may wake Its watch anon?

SPIRIT OF THE YEARS.

Nay. In the Foretime, even to the germ of Being
Nothing appears of shape to indicate
That cognizance has marshalled things terrene,
Or will (such is my thinking) in my span.
Rather they show that, like a knitter drowsed,
Whose fingers play in skilled unmindfulness,
The Will has woven with an absent heed
Since life first was; and ever will so weave.

It is something akin to a revelation for the attentive reader of these opening phrases to recognize therein the five unmistakable Schopenhauerian attributes of the Will :

1. The Will is One and Immanent ; for it is represented as the one and only source from which all life and activity are flowing, and its patterns underlie all mundane phenomena.

2. The Will is Autonomous ; determining everything, it is itself determined by nothing. Human

events are but the manifestations of its mysterious designs. No earthly power can swerve the pulsion of the Byss, which dominates all things by its clock-like laws.

3. The Will is Unconscious ; viewless and voice-less, the Turner of the Wheel works unconsciously, " an automatic sense, unweeting why or whence," " like a knitter drowsed, whose fingers play in skilled unmindfulness."

4. The Will is Aimless ; thinking on, it does not weigh its thought, and no answer is given to the question : " Why doth It so and so and ever so ? " If it has any aim at all, it is a listless aim.

5. The Will is Indestructible ; endless like the Wheel of Destiny it turns, it works eternal artistries in Circumstance. " The Will has woven with an absent heed since life first was, and ever will so weave."

These thoughts, admirable equally for their beauty and for their depth, visualized by a transcendent imagination, and compressed into less than two pages of poetry that grows upon one with its grandeur, represent the last stage of the intellectual develop-ment of Thomas Hardy and the final form into which his metaphysical thought has been cast. To value it correctly it will be necessary to review briefly his mental career and to mark the successive degrees by which he advanced to the ultimate expression of this world-view.

CHAPTER TWO

A METAPHYSICAL BIOGRAPHY OF
THOMAS HARDY

H ARDY RECOGNIZES at all times a monistic universe,
governed by one mysterious causality. This
vast governor or determinator he sees in every aspect
and every action of all phenomena, inanimate and
vital, but at different times his imagination clothes
this fundamental idea in different forms. His concepts
vary and develop in phraseology and connotation as
his thought matures, as his power of expression
increases, and as influences of other men's expressions
of kindred philosophies make themselves felt.

His earliest conception of the ultimate causality
in the universe takes the form of the idea of blind
Chance. He protests against this " crass casualty "
that need not have made life as miserable as it is, in
the early sonnet *Hap* (1866), which sounds the key-
note of the thought contained in all of his youthful
verse. Time, naturally, is conceived as the ally of
Chance, and together they are termed " purblind
Doomsters." The idea of fatalism, however, is hardly
emphasized here sufficiently to leave any abiding
impression upon the reader.

In the earliest novels, likewise, among the vast
welter of ideas that marks his period of experimen-
tation with his prose medium, his conception of

35

Chance and Circumstance as the powers that rule human destinies is easily the predominating one. In *Desperate Remedies* (1871), Cytherea is made to say—

" . . . Two disconnected events will fall strangely together by chance, and people scarcely notice the fact beyond saying, 'Oddly enough it happened that so and so were the same,' and so on. But when three such events coincide without any apparent reason for the coincidence, it seems as if there must be invisible means at work. . . ." [1]

and in his own person the author tells us that

Reasoning worldliness and infidelity . . . cannot repress on some extreme occasions the human instinct to pour out the soul to some Being or Personality, who in frigid moments is dismissed with the title of Chance, or at most Law. [2]

By far the most important early work as illustrating the sway exercised over Hardy's imagination and art by this conception is the generally vastly underrated novel *A Pair of Blue Eyes* (1873). [3] Here we find that he carries forward his idea of Chance, both in its expression and in its application to the development of his story. The following, for instance, is the extraordinary interpretation he gives to Aristotle's neat observation that " it is likely for many things to happen contrary to likelihood." [4]

---

[1] Chap. ix, 3. Note the highly artificial manipulation of incident throughout the book, e.g. Cytherea's unfortunate choice of a Friday for her marriage with Manston (chap. xii, 9).

[2] Chap. x, 7.

[3] Not only is it underrated as to its significance for the study of the development of the author's mind, but also as to its intrinsic artistic merit. It is almost incomprehensible that this novel, full of charm, pathos, deft manipulation of exciting incident, and truly overwhelming tragic irony at the close, can be habitually put into the same class as *Desperate Remedies*.

[4] *Poetics* xviii (1456–*a*).

Strange conjunctions of circumstance, particularly those of a trivial everyday kind, are so frequent in an ordinary life, that we grow used to their unaccountableness, and forget the question whether the very long odds against such juxtaposition is not almost a disproof of its being a matter of chance at all.[1]

The whole book develops into an orgy of tragic coincidences which batter the poor sufferers about with increasing savagery until the close, full of misery and irony. Even purely symbolic use of circumstance is employed, when, as the timid Elfride says to Knight, " Thou hast been my hope, and a strong tower for me against the enemy," the tower of Endelstow Church actually crumbles and falls before their eyes.[2] It is of some importance to note that circumstance, whether good or evil, is conceived by Hardy as an influence acting on characters and events from without themselves and not from within, as when Elfride feels that

There seemed to be a special facility offered her by a power external to herself in the circumstance that Mr. Swancourt had proposed to leave home the night previous to her wished-for day.[3]

Usually, however, the pranks of Chance are dreadful " Satires of Circumstance," as when Stephen recognizes a strangely cynical concomitant of his misery in the fact that his successful rival should be Knight, his former idol.[4] Time, the assisting agent of Chance in its devastating career, is ironically called " Time, the Improver," in *Desperate Remedies*,[5] and " Time, the Cynic," in *A Pair of Blue Eyes*.[6]

[1] Chap. x, 7.   [2] Chap. xxxi.   [3] Chap. xi.
[4] Chap. xxv.   [5] Chap. vii, 5.
[6] Chap. xxvii. Note that " Venus " in *Under the Greenwood Tree* (1872), (Pt. IV, chap. i), aids and abets Time and Chance in their sorry work.

Added to this dominant ground-tone of Circumstance, the reader of the early novels begins to distinguish murmurings of an even more tragic conception of the Power that shapes the course of human events [1] It is perhaps natural that fatalism, a motif that gradually usurped the place of Circumstance, should be found first expressed, not by the author himself, but by the rustics whom he delights to portray. It has often been said, and with a great deal of truth, that the old Germanic instinctive belief in an inscrutable and immovable Wyrd, or Destiny, still survives even among the more cultured inhabitants of the old Wessex kingdom, and that Hardy is reverting to the soil from which his fathers sprang when he displays deterministic tendencies. It may also be that his continual association with the country folk and his reporting of their speech and ideas gradually caused him to colour his own conceptions to match theirs. In *Desperate Remedies*, despite Mr. Springrove's flippant aphorism, " Fate's nothen beside a woman's schemen ! " [2] we find him delivering this remarkable discourse on death—

" . . . Ah, Baker, we see sudden death, don't we. But there's no difference in their nature between sudden death, and death of any other sort. There's no such thing as random snappen off of what was laid down to last longer. We only suddenly light upon an end—thoughtfully formed as any other—which has been existen at that very same point from the beginnen, though unseen by us to be so soon." [3]

---

[1] When Hardy's characters here refer to the orthodox conception of an all-wise and all-good Providence, it is nearly always with a palpable sneer, as when Providence seems to Manston " a mocking tormentor, laughing at him " (chap. xxi, 1), or when Mrs. Crickett responds to Mrs. Leat's hope that Providence " will settle it for the best, as He always do." . . . " Good people like you may say so, but I have always found Providence a different sort of feller " (chap. ix, 4).

[2] Chap. viii, 3.   [3] Chap. xxi, 1.

Metaphysical Biography of Thomas Hardy

In *Under the Greenwood Tree*, it is still the rustic characters and not the author of the book that give vent to their fatalistic instincts and convictions—

" . . . Ay, your pa'son comes by fate : 'tis heads or tails, like pitch-halfpenny, and no choosing ; so we must take en as he is, my sonnies, and thank God he's no worse, I suppose." [1]

By the time Hardy gets well into the writing of *A Pair of Blue Eyes*, however, the deterministic trend of thought bids fair to equal in significance the notion of Chance as the Prime Mover of the world. He introduces an analysis of Elfride's motives and actions as an attempt to " determine a resultant " as the natural effect of unchangeable conditions and causes.[2] More definite is his symbolic treatment of some of the characters. As the dainty Elfride may be said to represent, in herself, the volatility and capriciousness of Chance—although herself subject to Casualty in the form of tragic coincidences and to Fate in the form of heredity—so the black-robed, ominous figure of Mrs. Jethway, casting sinister shadows over even the brightest moments of the story, may be said to be an incarnation of the spirit of the Three Sisters or of the cankering fury of the ancient Nemesis. Throughout the action she calls attention to the hapless Elfride's early mistakes, and clearly suggests the ruin that will inevitably follow upon them ; and yet, considered by herself, the widow, in her grief for her son, is a sympathetic character. Likewise young Jethway's white tombstone is brought in continually as a symbol of Fate or Retribution, and is once said to stare in the faces of Knight and Elfie " like an avenging ghost." [3]

Throughout Hardy's early writings Nature in her

[1] Chap. ii. [2] Chap. xi. [3] Chap. xxxii.

various manifestations is also felt as a vast, vague Personality, bound up in some inscrutable manner with the human action of the stories. In *Desperate Remedies* the storm,[1] fire,[2] rain,[3] and ice [4] are dealt with as almost anthropomorphic cosmic agencies. Even more interesting and striking is the Nature that we encounter in *A Pair of Blue Eyes*. The personality of the Cliff Without a Name, coupled with the menacing attitude of the rainstorm and the wind, gives a tremendous cumulative effect to the two chapters that stand out as specimens of Hardy's most " dramatic " work.[5] As Knight clings for his life to the bare face of the almost perpendicular rock, the wind

tugged at his coat and lifted it. We are mostly accustomed to look upon all opposition which is not animate, as that of the stolid, inexorable hand of indifference, which wears out the patience more than the strength. Here, at any rate, hostility did not assume that slow and sickening form. It was a cosmic agency, active, lashing, eager for conquest, not an insensate standing in the way.

Meanwhile the sun presents a " red face, looking on with a drunken leer."

The following passage from the same chapter is a remarkable echo of the favourite Chance-doctrine, but coupled with an equally remarkable anticipation of the Nature that is presented in later works—

To those musing weather-beaten West-country folk who pass the greater part of their days and nights out of doors, Nature seems to have moods in other than a poetical sense : predilections for certain deeds at certain times, without any apparent law to govern or reason to account for them. She

[1] Chap. viii, 4.   [2] Chap. x, 2.
[3] Chap. xvi, 1.   [4] Chap. xiii, 1.
[5] Chap. xxi (" On thy cold grey stones, O Sea ! ") and chap. xxii (" A Woman's Way ").

is read as a person with a curious temper ; as one who does not scatter kindnesses and cruelties alternately, impartially, and in order, but heartless severities or overwhelming generosities in lawless caprice. Man's case is always that of the prodigal's favourite or the miser's pensioner. In her unfriendly moments there seems a feline fun in her tricks, begotten by a foretaste of her pleasure in swallowing the victim.

It is rather startling, perhaps, to find also in the very early works the clearest foreshadowings of the vast conception of the Immanent Will, under which all Hardy's previous visualizations of the One Causality are united in *The Dynasts* ;—but note how the idea is approached in passages like the following, in which outer nature and human personalities are united as one vital phenomenon—

The gentle sounds around them from the hills, the plains, the distant town, the adjacent shore, the water heaving at their side, the kiss, and the long kiss, were all " many a voice of one delight," and in union with each other.[1]

Even more significant is the author's comment on all the various personalities that Manston observes going about their business in the Strand—

Each and all were alike in this one respect, that they followed a solitary trail like the inwoven threads which form a banner, and all were equally unconscious of the significant whole they collectively showed forth.[2]

The group of novels which represents the product of the transitional decade beginning with *Far from the Madding Crowd* (1874) on the whole presents Hardy's nature-concepts in the strongest light,

[1] *Desperate Remedies*, chap. iii, 2.
[2] *Ibid.*, chap. xvi, 4. Vague hints of this conception can also be discovered in *A Pair of Blue Eyes*, chap. xiii, and in *The Trumpet-Major*, chap. xii.

although it also throws some illumination over the gradually fading personifications of Chance and Time, over the ever present ground-tone of Fatalism, and over the incessantly developing and maturing idea of the Immanent Will as the summation of all activity, the " Ding-an-sich " of the material and metaphysical universe.

On a clear night the twinkling of all the stars seems to Hardy to be " but throbs of one body, timed by a common pulse,"[1] and the dismal fog that comes down upon Joseph Poorgrass and his cart in the most dismal section of the story, is felt unmistakably to be Nature's silent commentary on the course of events—

> It was a sudden overgrowth of atmospheric fungi which had their roots in the neighbouring sea, and by the time that horse, man, and corpse entered Yalbury Great Wood, these silent workings of an invisible hand had reached them, and they were completely enveloped.[2]

To most people, Nature-personality in Hardy means just one theme in one of the novels : Edgon Heath in *The Return of the Native* (1878). Certainly nowhere else, in or out of Hardy, has this particular concept found more memorable setting and expression. The imposing first chapter gives not only the sombre background, but ushers in with an impressive dignity the real protagonist of the tragedy. Later the poly-phonic music of the heath, played upon by the wind, is described as the wildly rhetorical voice of this august character, of which Eustacia's sighs are a homogeneous part.[3] Throughout the book, except in those passages in which the grim heath " reduces

---

[1] *Far from the Madding Crowd*, chap. ii.   [2] Chap. xlii.
[3] *The Return of the Native*, book i, chap. vi.

to insignificance by its seamed and antique features the wildest turmoil " [1] of the human action, Nature is felt to reflect or to control the disastrous course of events. As the final catastrophe approaches, she puts on appropriate garb : the stormy heath is felt to be alive with the mighty forces that play in it. Possibly the greatest example in modern literature of the portrayal of the union between natural forces and human destinies is the passage from which the following extract is taken—

Skirting the pool she followed the path towards Rainbarrow, occasionally stumbling over twisted furze-roots, tufts of rushes, or oozing lumps of fleshy fungi, which at this season lay scattered about the heath like the rotten liver and lungs of some colossal animal. The moon and stars were closed up by cloud and rain to the point of extinction. It was a night which led the traveller's thoughts to dwell instinctively on nocturnal scenes of disaster in the chronicles of the world, or on all that is terrible and dark in history and legend—the last plague of Egypt, the destruction of Sennacherib's host, the agony in Gethsemane.

Eustacia at length reached the Rainbarrow, and stood still there to think. Never was harmony more perfect between the chaos of her mind and the choas of the world without. [2]

Even inanimate objects sometimes are invested with striking personal attributes, as when, in *Two on a Tower* (1882), a cottage with its single light appears to the nocturnal traveller " like a one-eyed creature watching him from an ambush." [3] In this novel also, at a rather tense moment in the story, to Lady Constantine

. . . The apocalyptic effect of the scene surrounding her was, indeed, not inharmonious, and afforded an appropriate background to her intentions. [4]

---

[1] *The Return of the Native*, book v, chap. ii. [2] Book v, chap. vii.
[3] *Two on a Tower*, chap. iii. [4] Chap. xvi.

In the same chapter the wind, "with the determination of a conscious agent," tears off the dome of Smithin's observatory, and then "rubs past them like a fugitive." [1]

Up to the writing of *The Mayor of Casterbridge* (1886), the theme of Nature as the Ultimate Causality is easily the predominating one. Traces of the earlier conception of Chance are not lacking, however, as when, for instance, the "sorcery of accident" is made to twist about the story of the elusive Ethelberta,[2] and when in *The Return of the Native* the dreadful night of the sixth of November is marked by a tragic, but none the less chanceful, concurrence of events. In the short story *Fellow-Townsmen* [3]

The events that had, as it were, dashed themselves together into one half-hour of this day showed that curious refinement of cruelty in their arrangement which often proceeds from the bosom of the whimsical god at other times known as blind Circumstance.

To St. Clare in *Two on a Tower* the "impishness of Circumstance was newer than it would have been to a philosopher of threescore-and-ten," [4] and Time, likewise, "brought about his revenges" upon poor Viviette.[5]

The feeling of fatalism also runs through the works of this period, although it, again, recedes before the more arresting Nature-characterizations with which the author is obsessed. An avenging Nemesis seems to drive onward the tragic course of events after Bathsheba's thoughtless sending of the foolish valentine to Boldwood, in *Far from the*

---

[1] Note also that in *Interlopers at the Knap* (1884), chap. i (in *Wessex Tales*), the raw breeze brings "a snore from the wood as if Skrymir the Giant were sleeping there."

[2] *The Hand of Ethelberta*, 1876, chap. xlv.

[3] 1880, in *Wessex Tales*.   [4] Chap. ix.   [5] Chap. xli.

Madding Crowd, and the white face of the dead Fanny Robin chastizes the spirit of her successful but miserable rival " with all the merciless rigor of the Mosaic law : ' Burning for burning ; wound for wound ; strife for strife.' " [1] Eustacia Vye feels at the end that her sad lot is really the result of a destiny beyond her control.[2] Here, however, Fate is conceived as Heaven, or Providence, and the question is carried over into the battle-ground of religion. The Supreme Power,[3] or the " colossal Prince of the World "[4] is blamed for the cruel obstructiveness of all the things that break the wings of the heroine's soul.[5] Even when dealing with the more submissive character of Clym, the novelist finds it impossible to refrain from some extremely biting ironical remarks that present the Higher Power as anything but a beneficent deity—

He did sometimes think that he had been ill-used by fortune, so far as to say that to be born is a palpable dilemma, and that instead of men aiming to advance in life with glory they should calculate how to retreat out of it without shame. But that he and his had been sarcastically and pitilessly handled in having such irons thrust into their souls he did not maintain long. It is usually so, except with the sternest of men. Human beings, in their generous endeavour to construct a hypothesis that shall not degrade a First Cause, have always hesitated to conceive a dominant power of lower moral quality than their own ; and, even while they sit down and weep by the waters of Babylon, invent excuses for the oppression which prompts their tears.[6]

The Mayor of Casterbridge (1886) represents the culmination of Hardy's instinctive and unselfconscious development of the fatalistic and retributive-justice

---

[1] Chap. xliii.   [2] *The Return of the Native*, Part V, chap. vii.
[3] Part IV, chap. iii.   [4] Part IV, chap. viii.   [5] Part V, chap. vii.
[6] Part VI, chap. i. Note also " Heaven's persistent irony," in *Far from the Madding Crowd*, chap. viii ; and the discouraging attitude of Providence towards Troy's good intentions, chap. xlvi.

ideas that he inherited from the Hebrew lawgivers, the Greek thinkers, and the ancient Germanic heroes. Here we find the primitive concepts in their purest, starkest form. Like *The Return of the Native* it is full of echoes of old Wessex superstitions, beliefs, and customs, such as Henchard's interview with the " weather-caster," [1] and the " Skimmity-Ride." The old Roman amphitheatre, used for the setting of several of the more memorable scenes, is rich in its suggestion of a significant past ; " it might have been called the spittoon of the Foteens." [2] The possibility of the closest analogies between the characterizations and movement of the story and many an ancient Nemesis-tragedy has already been pointed out. The book can also be considered as an illustration of the Old-Testament doctrine of Inevitable Retribution, and when so considered will be found to present a large mass of suggestive material. There are a large number of Scriptural references and quotations, a criticism of the Hebrew morality expressed in Psalm 109, and there is also discoverable a most striking analogy between the stories of Saul and David and of Henchard and Farfrae—an analogy whose details will be manifest even to the casual reader. The Biblical and the Greek doctrines here reflected both express Hardy's determinism in its simplest and most colourful form.

The strong dash of idealistic philosophy that was ushered in by the novel of the following year, *The Woodlanders*, completely transfigured the novelist's expression of his outlook upon the world. Hereafter he is no longer content to echo and re-echo ancient conceptions with hints of the ancients' manner of literary expression ; hereafter he takes his hints from

[1] Chap. xxvi.   [2] Chap. xi.

the most modern metaphysical thinkers. He turns from an instinctive fatalist into a conscious philosophical artist. In *The Woodlanders*, however, he has not yet succeeded in uniting the new conceptions to the older machinery of its predecessors ; at its best the idealism found there is but imperfectly and crudely united with Time and Chance,[1] Circumstance,[2] Determinism and Fate,[3] and Nature.[4] Only one remarkable foreshadowing of the Immanent-Will-idea as the union of all vital phenomena must be noted—

Hardly anything could be more isolated or more self-contained than the lives of these two walking here in the lonely antelucan hour, when gray shades, material and mental, are so very gray. And yet, looked at in a certain way, their lonely courses formed no detached design at all, but were part of the pattern in the great web of human doings then weaving in both hemispheres, from the White Sea to Cape Horn.[5]

In *Tess* (1891), although he still expresses his notion of the Dominant Causality as Time,[6] as relentless Nemesis,[7] or Fate,[8] and as Nature (as seen in the

[1] Chap. ii. [2] Chaps. xii and xvi. [3] Chap. xv.
[4] Especially chapter xliv. [5] Chap. iii.
[6] The first American edition of the book anathematized *Time the Archsatirist* at the close, instead of the more familiar *President of the Immortals*.
[7] Note that the book opens with a single seemingly insignificant incident, which, however, sets in motion the subsequent endless chain of tragic causes and consequences.
[8] It is rather striking that in the course of the story both Tess and Clare develop intellectually into determinists : " Tess was now carried along upon the wings of the hours, without the sense of a will. The word had been given ; the number of the day written down. Her naturally bright intelligence had begun to admit the fatalistic convictions common to field-folk and those who associate more extensively with natural phenomena than with their fellow-creatures ; and she accordingly drifted into that passive responsiveness to all things her lover suggested, characteristic of the frame of mind " (chap. xxxii).
" Mr. Clare's creed of determinism was such that it almost amounted to a vice, and quite amounted, on its negative side, to a renunciative philosophy which had cousinship with that of Schopenhauer and Leopardi " (chap. xxv).

whole Froom Valley dairy-farm episode), Hardy's
favourite vehicle for the conveyance of his intellectual
convictions is the idea, or associations of ideas, grouped
by Schopenhauer under the term " Will." [1]   The
Will is called by that name in only one of the following typical extracts, but the conception is unmistakably
the same Schopenhauerian one in each—

> She had consented.   She might as well have agreed at
> first.   The " appetite for joy " which stimulates all creation ;
> that tremendous force which sways humanity to its purpose,
> as the tide sweeps the helpless weed, was not to be controlled
> by a vague sense of self-abnegation. [2]

> The irresistible, universal, automatic tendency to find
> enjoyment, which pervades all life, from the meanest to the
> highest, had at length mastered her. [3]

> The unpremeditated gravitation of the two into one . . .
> was based upon a more stubborn and resistless tendency than a
> whole heap of so-called practicalities. [4]

> Tess and Clare unconsciously studied each other, even
> balanced on the edge of a passion, yet apparently keeping out
> of it.   All the while they were none the less converging,
> under the force of irresistible law, as surely as two streams
> in a vale. [5]

> So the two forces were at work here as everywhere, the
> inherent will to enjoy, and the circumstantial will against
> enjoyment. [6]

In *Jude* (1895) there are many traces of both,
" Bejahung des Willens zum Leben," and " Ver-
neinung des Willens zum Leben," as expressed in
the last quotation from *Tess*.   The physician, in

---

[1] There is a remarkable anticipation of the Schopenhauerian phraseology
in *Two on a Tower*, chap. x : " The strenuous wish to live and behold
the new phenomenon, supplanting the utter weariness of existence that
he had heretofore experienced, lent him a new vitality.

[2] Chap. xxviii.   [3] Chap. xiv.   [4] Chap. xxii.
[5] Chap. xvli.   [6] Chap. xliii.

explanation of the suicide of Little Father Time, says
" it is the beginning of the coming universal wish
not to live," [1] and the author thus comments upon
Arabella's fatal attraction for the hero—

This seemed to care little for his reason and his will
nothing for his so-called elevated intentions, and moved him
along, as a violent schoolmaster a schoolboy he has seized by
the collar, in a direction which tended towards the embrace
of a woman for whom he had no respect, and whose life had
nothing in common with his own except locality. [2]

The Immanent Will is here definitely conceived
both as " the will in nature " and as the " one
mysterious causality " ; Sue's imaginings approach
very closely to the wisdom of the Spirit of the Years
in *The Dynasts*, when she supposes that

. . . the first Cause worked automatically like a somnam-
bulist, and not reflectively, like a sage ; that at the framing
of the terrestrial conditions there seemed never to have been
contemplated such a development of emotional perceptiveness
among the creatures subject to these conditions as that reached
by thinking and educated humanity. [3]

We can thus trace through the novels the general
development, with many overlappings of ideas, of
Hardy's expression of a consistent world-view through
the notions of Chance and Time, Circumstance, Fate,
Nature, Providence, Nemesis, and Will, tinged with
metaphysical idealism.   This last and definitive conception can be seen emerging out of his vaguer former
deterministic notions in such a poem as *He Wonders*

[1] Part VI, chap. ii.
[2] Part I, chap. vii.
[3] Part VI, chap. iii.   The older ideas are still discoverable in *Jude*.
Circumstance, Fate (in the female guise of Arabella), and Nature (here
degraded from the wholesome sheepfold or dairy-farm to the disgusting
atmosphere of the piggery).

About Himself,[1] written at about the time when *Jude*
was taking shape (1893)—

> No use hoping, or feeling vexed,
> Tugged by a force above or under
> Like some fantocine, much I wonder
> What I shall find me doing next !
>
> Shall I be rushing where bright eyes be ?
> Shall I be suffering sorrows seven ?
> Shall I be watching the stars of heaven,
> Thinking one of them looks like thee ?
>
> Part is mine of the general Will,
> Cannot my share in the sun of sources
> Bend a digit the poise of forces,
> And a fain desire fulfil ?

By the year 1901 he seems to have been already
engaged in his magnum opus, the first instalment of
which was to startle the world three years later.   At
any rate, he published in this year a poem that epitomizes the whole intellectual plot of *The Dynasts*.
ʼΑΓΝΩΣΤΩ, ΘΕΩ,,[2] for all its suggestion of the
earlier personal traits in the character of the Prime
Mover as first conceived by Hardy, is a full and clear
expression of the high-lights, at least, of Hardy's final
conception of the force that sways the universe—and
there is in addition that touch of melioristic optimism
at the end that we shall find to be the redeeming
feature of his otherwise hopeless world—

> Long have I framed weak phantasies of Thee,
>   O Willer masked and dumb !
> Who makest Life become,—
> As though by labouring all-unknowingly,
>   Like one whom reveries numb.

How much of consciousness informs Thy will
    Thy biddings, as if blind,
    Of death-inducing kind,
Nought shows to us ephemeral ones who fill
    But moments in Thy mind.

Perhaps Thy ancient rote-restricted ways
    Thy ripening rule transcends ;
    That listless effort tends
To grow percipient with advance of days,
    And with percipience mends.

For, in unwonted purlieus, far and nigh
    At whiles or short or long,
    May be discerned a wrong
Dying as of self-slaughter ; whereat I
    Would raise my voice in song.

To emphasize the unity of Hardy's basic thought throughout his work in prose and verse, one might finally compare the fundamental ideas of *The Convergence of the Twain* [1] and of *Hap*.[2] The attitude towards life is identical in both poems, and the subject-matter is similar, but to what an extent has a life of philosophic study and meditation, and of practice in writing developed, nay, transfigured the expression of his attitude !

One can hardly expect from a poet—even a cosmic poet—the observation that " Will is the Thing-in-itself," expressed in so many words ; but if this definite philosophic concept is to be found anywhere expressed in the language and imagery of poetry, it is found in this wonderful section of the " Fore-Scene " to *The Dynasts* (1903), in which " the anatomy of the Will " is for the first time visualized—

The nether sky opens, and Europe is disclosed as a prone and emaciated figure, the Alps shaping like a backbone, and

[1] 1914. In *Satires of Circumstance* (hereafter abbreviated *SC*).
[2] 1866, *WP*.

the branching mountain-chains like ribs, the peninsular plateau of Spain forming a head. Broad and lengthy lowlands stretch from the north of France across Russia like a grey-green garment hemmed by the Ural mountains and the glistening Arctic Ocean.

The point of view then sinks downwards through space, and draws near to the surface of the perturbed countries, where the peoples, distressed by events, which they did not cause, are seen writhing, crawling, heaving, and vibrating in their various cities and nationalities.

SPIRIT OF THE YEARS (TO THE SPIRIT OF THE PITIES).
> *As key-scene of the whole, I first lay bare*
> *The Will-webs of thy fearful questioning;*
> *For know that of my antique privileges*
> *This gift to visualize the Mode is one*
> *(Though by exhaustive strain and effort only,)*
> *See, then, and learn, ere my power pass again.*

A new and penetrating light descends on the spectacle, enduing men and things with a seeming transparency, and exhibiting as one organism the anatomy of life and movement in all humanity and vitalized matter included in the display.

SPIRIT OF THE PITIES (after a pause).
> *Amid this scene of bodies substantive*
> *Strange waves I sight like winds grown visible,*
> *Which bear men's forms on their innumerous coils,*
> *Twining and serpenting round and through.*
> *Also retracting threads like gossamers—*
> *Except in being irresistible—*
> *Which complicate with some, and balance all.*

SPIRIT OF THE YEARS.
> *These are the Prime Volitions,—fibrils, veins,*
> *Will-tissues, nerves, and pulses of the Cause,*
> *That heave throughout the Earth's compositure.*
> *Their sum is like the lobule of a Brain*
> *Evolving always that it wots not of;*

Metaphysical Biography of Thomas Hardy

A Brain whose whole connotes the Everywhere,
And whose procedure may but be discerned
By phantom eyes like ours; the while unguessed
Of those it stirs, who (even as ye do) dream
Their motions free, their orderings supreme;
Each life apart from each, with power to mete
Its own day's measures; balanced, self-complete;
Though they subsist but atoms of the One
Labouring through all, divisible from none;
But this no further now. Deem yet man's deeds self-done.

The anatomy of the Immanent Will disappears.

CHAPTER THREE

"WHAT OF THE IMMANENT WILL?"

APPARENTLY THE WEAKEST, and yet perhaps the strongest and altogether most obvious link in the chain of Schopenhauer's thoughts is his assertion of the metaphysical oneness of the Will. He sees the underlying principle of the universe expanding and diversifying itself in a great number of ground-forms or objectifications, which, like Plato's ideas, are the eternal moulds of all things, independent of time and space, beyond the sphere of perception, absolutely stable and unchanging, always being and never becoming.[1] He sees each of these objectifications of the Will manifesting itself in myriads of individual things, each of which bearing the general outlines and chief characteristics of its " idea," without ever fully realizing it. But behind and beyond and at the base of this infinite multiplicity of things, he recognizes the One Will, manifesting its energy throughout the universe, and forming the bond of unity between all things.[2]

[1] Sch. i, 184 sqq.

[2] Schopenhauer is careful to explain that the Will is one, not in the sense in which an object is one, for the unity of the object can only be known through its juxtaposition to a possible multiplicity ; nor yet in the sense in which an idea is one, for the unity of the idea originates only in abstraction from a multiplicity. But it is one as that which lies outside of time and space, the *principium individuationis,* and is therefore beyond the possibility of all multiplicity.

" What of the Immanent Will ? "

Despite its objectification in the multiplicity of things the Will itself remains forever indivisible. There is not a smaller part of the Will in the stone and a larger part in man, for the relation of part and whole belongs exclusively to space, and has no longer any meaning when we go beyond this form of perception. Nor is the One Will affected by the multiplicity of individual phenomena in each of its objectifications, that is, by the multitude of individuals in each form, for this multiplicity is directly conditioned by time and space, into which the Will itself cannot enter. The Will reveals itself as much and as completely in one oak as in millions of them. If, *per impossibile*, a single real existence, even the most insignificant, were to be entirely annihilated, the whole world would necessarily perish with it.[1]

The conception of the oneness of the Will leads Schopenhauer to a recognition of teleology in nature and the unity of all human events, which, as manifestations of the same fundamental energy, are not only connected by the law of causality, but bear the features of an essentially identical physiognomy. A true valuation of historical events and a demonstration of the essential unity between them requires poetical treatment in the best sense of the term. For history, considered merely as a recital of events in all their details, will always, and of necessity, be imperfect,

---

[1] Schopenhauer in this connection gives unqualified assent to the saying of Angelus Silesius, the mystic—

" Ich weiss, dass ohne mich Gott nicht ein Nu kann leben :
　Werd'ich zunicht', er muss vor Not den Geist aufgeben."

It is perhaps only because Schopenhauer tried to think what no mind can grasp, and to define what no language can express, that he loses himself in channels of reasoning where the laws of ordinary logic no longer hold sway. Otherwise the contradiction between the two cardinal concepts is obvious : The Will can never become object—and, the Will objectifies itself.

fragmentary, erroneous, and misleading, and it is a question whether the historical records of the past do not contain more error than truth. While history unfolds before our eyes the spectacle of uninterrupted change and teaches us that at every period of time there happened something different, philosophy maintains that this change is non-essential, and that at all times there was the same. The essence of human life is completely present in every event and, to be fully comprehended, requires only depth of perception. But history, in the narrow sense, attempts to communicate knowledge, not by depth of perception, but by length and breadth of description. It is the poet's eye that will discover that history after all on every page recounts the same thing, though in different forms. Its chapters are different only in names and dates ; the essential content is the same everywhere.[1] Whoever desires to know man in his inner nature will find that the works of the great poets present a far truer, more distinct picture, than mere historians can ever give. Paradoxical as it may sound, there is more truth in fiction than in the most faithful recital of events. It is significant that Schopenhauer in this connection quotes approvingly the words of a great poet who was a great historian also—

> " Was sich nie und nirgends hat begeben,
> Das allein veraltet nie."—SCHILLER.[2]

In the small sphere of an individual life, when described with truth, Schopenhauer finds the whole compass of human existence in all its form and subtilties : the excellence, the virtue, and even holiness of a few, the perversity, meanness, and knavery

[1] Sch. ii, 517 sqq.   [2] Sch. i, 326 sq.

of most, the dissolute profligacy of some. With regard to the ultimate significance of phenomena it is quite immaterial whether the objects of human actions are, relatively considered, trifling or important, whether they are farms or kingdoms. For all these things in themselves are without significance, and obtain it only in so far as the Will is moved by them. As a circle of one inch in diameter has precisely the same geometrical properties as a circle of forty million miles in diameter, so the events and the history of a village and the events and the history of a kingdom are essentially the same, and the true nature of mankind appears in the one with no less distinctiveness than in the other. Here as there and everywhere, it is the One Will manifesting itself.

It is in strictest harmony with the very genius of Schopenhauer's philosophy as well as in the line of an unavoidable logical conclusion from basic premises to deny the existence and operation of exterior forces exercising any influence upon the world. There is no room in his thought for a supramundane power, whether it be conceived as material or spiritual, conscious, unconscious, or superconscious. No First Cause, itself unmoved, can set in motion the clockwork of interjoined cause and effect. No Deity can superimpose his predestined decrees upon the course of human events. The whole conception of supramundanity is foreign to a system based on the idea of One Will objectifying itself in all things and forming the bond of unity between the multitude of diversified phenomena. It is utterly repugnant to its author. To admit the possibility of a transcendental force would be to destroy the unity of the world, flowing from the Oneness of the Will. Although Schopenhauer knows nothing about the term *monism*, which was of later invention, and very rarely uses the expression *immanent*, yet his whole philosophy is permeated by the conception of a monistic universe, based on the Immanence of the Will.

The old quest for a First Cause, externally conceived, springs, according to Schopenhauer, from a misconception of the law of causality, which has its proper sphere in the world of perception, where it supplies the principle of coherence between the different forms of matter and explains the succession of their appearance and disappearance in time and space. But to apply this law of causality to pure matter itself, as philosophers so frequently have done, and, instead of being content with the discovery of the cause of every phenomenon of the world, to ask for a cause of the world itself, entangles the mind in the inextricable meshes of a *regressus ad infinitum*. Such argumentation starts from the baseless assumption that existence is always preceded by non-existence ; that therefore from the fact of the existence of the world the fact of its previous non-existence may be inferred, as well as its transition from the state of non-existence to the state of existence, by its coming into being through the operation of some mysterious First Cause. Such reasoning, Schopenhauer says, always ends with the most " fearful inconsistency ; it does away entirely with the law of causality from which alone it drew its evidencing power, it stops at a First Cause and will go no further, and ends thus, as it were, by committing parricide, as the bees kill the drones after they have served their ends." The world, then, is in no way the result, or the creation, or the effect of any power outside of it, whether it be called the First Cause, or the Absolute, or God. There is nothing to be discovered beneath the maze of things but the energy of the Immanent Will.[1]

It is evident from these premises that Schopenhauer cannot assign to religion a very distinguished place in the general scheme of things. The reader may well be shocked by the frequent expressions of utter disdain in which he holds the outward manifestations of the religious life. Yet his attitude is not that of unqualified rejection.

The origin of religion as well as of philosophy he discovers in the innate metaphysical need of man, who, among all things, is the only one who wonders at his existence. The wisdom of nature speaks out of the peaceful glance of the brutes, for in them will and intellect are not so widely separated that they can be astonished at each other. Here the phenomenon is still firmly attached to the stem of nature from which it has come and is partaker of the omniscience of the great mother.[2] Only after the inner being of nature has ascended through the series of unconscious existences and the long line of animals does it at last attain to conscious reflection on the entrance of reason. Then it begins to marvel and asks what it itself may be, as Aristotle says in the beginning of his Metaphysics : Διὰ γὰρ τὸ θαυμάζειν οἱ ἄνθρωποι καὶ νῦν καὶ τὸ πρῶτον ἤρξαντο φιλοσοφεῖν.

In particular it is the fact that reasoning man finds himself face to face with the strange phenomenon of death and is profoundly impressed by the consciousness of universal suffering and misery in life, that this metaphysical astonishment is greatly deepened and sharpened. If our life were endless and painless, Schopenhauer thinks, it would perhaps occur to no

[1] Sch. ii, 57 sq.　　　　[2] Sch. ii, 184 sqq.

one to ask why the world exists ; everything would just be taken as a matter of course. The interest which religious systems inspire has its strongest hold in the dogma of some kind of existence after death ; and although the most recent systems (Judaism and Christianity) seem to make the existence of their gods the main points, and defend this most zealously, yet in reality this is only because they have connected their special dogma of immortality with it, and regard the one as inseparable from the other. For, says Schopenhauer, if one could establish the doctrine of immortality in some other way, the lively zeal for the gods would at once cease, and it would give way to complete indifference if, conversely, the absolute impossibility of immortality were proven. " But if one could demonstrate that continued existence after death is incompatible with the existence of gods, because, let us say, it presupposes originality of being, the most ardent religionists would unhesitatingly sacrifice all gods to their own immortality and become zealous for atheism." [1]

The value of religion, then, consists in its ability to satisfy the metaphysical need of man, once awakened, in the only form in which the vast majority will ever be able to apprehend truth, the form of allegory and myth. In this respect religion is, though not the truth, yet the best substitute for truth the ignorant can grasp. It is as useful to the unphilosophical multitude as a wooden leg is to the invalid who has lost his real leg. Every religion is true and false at the same time. It is true when taken *sensu allegorico*, as the mythical and pictorial representation of metaphysical facts and conditions. It is a tissue of absurdities and lies when the historical

[1] Sch. ii, 192.

frame and the allegorical garb of its doctrines are taken *sensu proprio,* and paraded as actual facts. Christianity, in particular, replacing as it did the shallow Græco-Roman polytheism and introducing into the intellectual life of the Western world the imperishable elements of truth contained in the ancient Hindu religion, has served a useful purpose in upholding the ideals of justice, charity, compassion, reconciliation, love of enemies, humility, patience, self-denial, faith, and hope. Its very foundation is the doctrine that the world is evil and in need of redemption. It accordingly teaches contempt of the world, self-abnegation, chastity, abandonment of the individual will, and a resolute turning away from life and its treacherous joys.[1] It points out the sanctifying power of suffering, and its symbol is an instrument of torture.[2]

It is true that this earnest and only correct view of life was known in Asia thousands of years before the Christian era and at the present time is entertained by many entirely independently of all Christian influences ; but for the nations of Europe it was indeed a great and new revelation. Christianity is infinitely better than Islam, founded on the Koran, " that bad book," in which Schopenhauer professes not to have been able to discover a single decent thought.[3] It ranks infinitely higher than `Judaism which has poisoned the thoughts of men with the absurd doctrine that man was the work of a foreign will,[4] and created by him out of nothing. While Judaism is realistic and optimistic, and with marvellous success has fostered in its adherents the will to live, Chris-

---

[1] " Abwendung vom Leben und seinen truegerischen Freuden," Sch. i, 459.
[2] Sch. i, 417 sqq.   [3] Sch. ii, 186.   [4] Sch. i, 497 ; ii, 595.

tianity is thoroughly idealistic and pessimistic and tends toward resignation and the denial of the will to live.[1]

However, to attain these beneficent ends it must be rightly understood and the emphasis must be placed where it belongs, on the spiritual doctrines of sin and redemption, and not on the events connected with the life and the death of its founder and the ridiculous miracle-stories with which its written records are teeming. This, unfortunately, is done by the representatives of Christianity. At all times there have been unscrupulous men who engaged in the profitable business of exploiting the metaphysical need of man. These monopolists and farmers-general (" Generalpaechter ") of religion, the priests, have by their stubborn insistence on the literal interpretation of biblical allegories so distorted Christianity that it has become the most revolting doctrine imaginable. Its history has been so marked by crusades, religious wars, executions of heretics and dissenters, persecutions, cursings, anathematizations, and other bloody manifestations of bigotry and intolerance, that it can no longer support the claim of being the basis for the moral life of mankind, but has instead become the most shockingly immoral religion of all times. The priests, " diese Pfaffen aller Farben "[2] have accomplished it, that the saying is only too true : Behind the cross there stands the devil.[3] Schopenhauer considers it no less than criminal that priests under the protection of the State should have the prerogative to instruct children in their articles of faith and by inculcating their superstitions into the young minds so firmly, deeply, and earnestly, as to

[1] Sch., *Parerga und Paralipomena,* ii, 382.
[2] Sch. ii, 187 ; *Parerga,* ii, 414.
[3] Sch., *Parerga,* " Ueber Religion," 338–415.

bring about a partial paralysis of the brain which, except in cases of exceptional intellectual elasticity, will incapacitate them for all time to think independently.[1]   It evokes not only his ire, but his most sarcastic ridicule, that the representatives of such a corrupted Christianity should have the arrogance to send " Saxon journeymen-tailors and Moravian linen-weavers " to India to convert the " heathen ! "   What an idea, to expect that " the original wisdom of humanity (die Urweisheit des Menschengeschlechts) could be dislodged by the events of Galilee ! "   In spite of his frequently expressed admiration for the intellectual and moral endowments of the English nation, he observes with dismay that this nation is foremost in missionary enterprise and commits, as it were, the unpardonable sin of firmly holding fast to belief in a god.[2]

Aside from the distorting of its true doctrines by the dogmaticians, Schopenhauer discovers one particularly serious defect in Christianity, even when rightly understood : the utter lack of just consideration for animals.   No matter how strongly one may disagree with him in other respects, every reader of his books must be deeply touched and quite carried along by the eloquence of his earnest pleading for justice toward " our dumb brothers."   Instead of recognizing the " eternal essence"' (das ewige Wesen) as manifesting itself no less in animals than in us, Christianity has torn man away from the animal world, erected a barrier between the two, and, supported by the Old Testament doctrine, that man should rule over the beasts of the field, and the fowl of the air, and the fishes of the sea, has carefully worked out an elaborate code for the protection of man, and

[1] Sch. ii, 184 sqq.   [2] Sch. i, 459 ; *Parerga* ii, 340 sq.

delivered the animals defenceless and helpless into
his hands. How much higher, in this respect, is
the viewpoint of the ancient Hindu religion ! The
Hindu and Buddhist believes in the " Mahavakya,"
—the great word,—" Tat-twam asi," that is, " This
is you ! " and he pronounces it over every animal to
remind himself of the inner identity of the real
essence in them and in him.[1] In " uncircumcized
Asia," a man will show gratitude to the gods, not
by blabbing a Te Deum, but by going to the market-
place and buying birds and then proceeding to the
city gates to open the cage.[2] " Compare with this the
revolting cruelty, crying to heaven, with which our
Christian rabble treats the animals ; without any
purpose—and laughingly—killing them, or maiming
them, or tormenting them, and ill-using and over-
working in their old age even those of them who,
like the horses, have been his supporters, in order to
crush the last remnant of marrow out of their poor
bones, till they finally succumb under his merciless
blows. Truly, one might say : Men are the devils
of the earth, and the animals the tormented souls ! "[3]
Schopenhauer is an ardent advocate of the Societies
for the Prevention of Cruelty to Animals, and highly
commends the English, " the most sensitive and
merciful nation of all," for having been the pioneer
in the organization of this and kindred humanitarian
movements. The utter contempt in which he holds
physicians is probably traceable to his violent and
passionate objection to vivisection as practised by
them.

However, unalterably as Schopenhauer is opposed
to every religious conception of a " foreign will "
creating, preserving, or governing the universe, he is

[1] *Parerga* ii, 392.   [2] ii, 389.   [3] ii, 390.

equally far removed from the theories of materialism. It is interesting to note that his aversion to materialism grew in intensity with the passing years, as he himself more clearly surveyed the bearings of the doctrine of the Immanent Will. While his first books display a willingness to discuss calmly the underlying principles with the advocates of the naturalistic view, his later writings are sprinkled with acrid invective against " the stupid materialists," whom he hates with as perfect a hatred as he does priests, professors of philosophy, and Hegel.[1]

Materialism, he holds, is based on the πρῶτον ψεῦδος of confounding matter in the metaphysical sense with the " Stoff," as it appears in a distinct form and with fixed attributes in the world of phenomena.[2] It is an outgrowth of realism, and in " its incredible ignorance of first principles " overlooks the fundamental fact that matter, as perceived by our senses, cannot be the thing-in-itself. Nothing indeed could be more clumsy (" täppisch ") than to take the object without examination as a given thing and not to reflect that the subject is its necessary condition.[3] Thus materialism can be termed the philosophy of the subject forgetting itself in the process of its mental operations. For the assertion that " I am only a modification of matter," must be corrected by the other, that " all matter exists only in my perception." The history of materialism demonstrates that materialism always flourishes in intellectually backward times, and is an unfailing sign of the deterioration of thought. It is always accompanied by its faithful comrade, bestiality, and thus undermines the moral structure of the world.[4]

[1] Sch. ii, 59.
[3] Sch. ii, 21 sq.
[2] Sch. ii, 368.
[4] Sch. ii, 372.

It is evident, then, that, though Schopenhauer's view of the universe as the manifestation of the One and Immanent Will is essentially monistic, yet he does not subscribe to materialistic monism. He recognizes the existençe of basic spiritual elements as underlying all phenomena. His world-view is Idealistic Monism.

That Hardy's world-view also is Idealistic Monism is evidenced by the frequency with which the epithet " Immanent " is applied to the Will. While Schopenhauer prefers to designate the Fundamental Energy " One," because he sees it primarily as all-embracing and all-pervading, indivisible and complete in every phenomenon, Hardy usually employs for the expression of the same general idea the term " Immanent," because he is primarily interested in excluding every conception of an exterior force essentially different from the universe and outside of it. Immanent Will is interior energy, thus all movement and development in the world is self-movement and self-development. The conceptions of oneness and immanence in the Schopenhauer–Hardy cosmology are inseparably bound together : each is a necessary corollary and consequence of the other, and both are of equal importance in the work of each of the two writers.

Sometimes Hardy simply designates the Will as " The Immanent " or " Immanence," as " The Immanence that urges all,"[1] or—

> *O Immanence, that reasonest not*
> *In putting forth all things begot. . . .*[2]

or, as the Spirit of the Years explains Waterloo—

> *So hath the Urging Immanence used to-day*
> *His inadvertent might to field this fray.*[3]

---

[1] *Dynasts*, I, 2, v.   [2] After-Scene.   [3] III, 7, viii.

66

It is of particular significance that Hardy frequently employs the colourless pronoun "It," or "That," without applying to it any qualitative or limiting attribute, in designating the Will. The use of these indefinite neutral words indicates the poet's intention to present the Will as indefinable, in so far as definition implies comparison or contrast with other things. The Will is essentially identical with all things, and is therefore beyond the sphere in which one phenomenon is limited by others. It is thus unlimited in the fullest sense of the term.

That the Will is conceived as the creative principle of the universe is suggested by Hardy's use of the term "inbrooding Will." [1] That it is the organizing principle seems to be indicated by the image of the "Weaver," linking all phenomena together in its vast designs. Before the birth of Napoleon it "weaves Its web in that Ajaccian womb," [2] thus fitting the life of the conqueror and all the consequences resulting from his actions into its general scheme of things, and using the figure of the tyrant only as one particular thread in the enormous tapestry of events.

As the conception of the Immanent Will leads Schopenhauer to the teleological view of nature, so in the thought of Hardy the idea of the fundamental identity of outer nature with human nature is closely allied to the conception of the Will as the organizing and unifying principle of the universe. As early as the writing of *The Return of the Native* he had shown his fondness for endowing even inanimate objects with personalities and making them as essential parts of his stories as the human agents. Nature with Hardy is not an exterior influence, such as Wordsworth's beneficent Nature, but is an inherent con-

[1] *Dynasts*, I, 5, iv.   [2] After-Scene.

dition, itself governed by the same forces that sway the destinies of mankind. This view of Nature as a puppet of the Will, like man, is perfectly expressed in the poem *The Subalterns* (*PP*). The lyric poet often mourns his change in attitude toward the Great Mother, as well as Her indifference to him,[1] and frequently complains of what seems to be Her heartlessness.[2] In *The Sleep-Walker* (*PP*) she is, curiously enough, identified with both God and the Will. The voices of outer nature, as in the prose stories, accompany the action of many of the poems ; sometimes accentuating it by their harmony with the mood of the situation, sometimes driving the point home by means of ironic contrast.[3] Even in the recollection of a picture which would ordinarily be regarded as beautiful, a natural phenomenon is presented as reflecting, illustrating, and harmonizing with the tragic mood of the poet, as he relates—

> I climbed to the crest,
>   And, fog-festooned
> The sun lay west
>   Like a crimson wound :
>
> Like that wound of mine
>   Of which none knew,
> For I'd given no sign
>   That it pierced me through.[4]

In *The Dynasts* also Nature is felt as an essential part of the great web of the Will. During the Battle of Ulm, " the stream, which is swollen by the rainfall

---

[1] E.g. *To Outer Nature* (*WP*).
[2] See *To a Motherless Child* (*WP*).
[3] In *The Voice of Things* (*MV*) the sounds of nature are at first in harmony, then (in stanza 3) in ironic contrast to the human feeling.
[4] *The Wound* (*MV*).

and rasped by the storm, seems wanly to sympathize," [1]
and a particularly ghastly effect is achieved by the
following touch added to a most vivid description of
the frightful slaughter at Vimiero : " A dust is raised
by this ado, and moans of men and shrieks of horses
are heard.   Close by the carnage the little Maceira
river continues to trickle unconcernedly to the sea." [2]

As the creative principle, the Will is at the bottom
of all the great world-movements, upheavals of
nations, and careers of dynasties.   Wars are but
" whirlwinds of the Will," [3] the Grand Army of
France in retreat is moved by " That within it," [4]
and the Spirit of the Years, in introducing the second
visualization of the Will, declares, that it shows " the
all-inhering Power," which, by working from within,
determines the course of events.   And so it does
not behoove the Spirits of the Pities, much less men,
to criticize the Will according to man-made ethical
standards.   It stands above all the categories of
human thought, completely beyond the conceptions
of good and evil, of the desirable and undesirable,
of joy and pain.   The Pities, and men likewise, are
warned not to be " critical of That which was before
and shall be after " them.[5]

As the great world-movements are manifestations
of the Immanent Will, so every individual action
flows from the universal " inhering Power."   It
" instilled large potencies " into Napoleon's idiosyn-
crasies,[6] it is the creator of each individual character
and directs its course.   Separate lives are but atoms
of the One that labours through all, divisible from
none.[7]   Great men at critical moments become mere

[1] *Dynasts*, I, 4, iv.   [2] II, 2, vii.   [3] III, 7, iv.
[4] III, 1, ix.   [5] I, 5, iv.   [6] Fore-Scene.
[7] This conception of the relation of the Will to individuals as of the whole
to its parts is a slight variation from Schopenhauer.

mouthpieces and give utterance to the tendencies of the Will, as when Pitt, hailed as the saviour of Britain, responds with these words—[1]

> My lords and gentlemen :—you have toasted me
> As one who has saved England and her cause.
> I thank you, gentlemen, unfeignedly.
> But—no man has saved England, let me say :
> England has saved herself, by her exertions :
> She will, I trust, save Europe by her example !

The Spirit of the Years comments as follows—

> *Those words of this man Pitt—his last large words,*
> *As I may prophesy—that ring to-night*
> *In their first mintage to the feasters here,*
> *Will spread with ageing, lodge, and crystallize,*
> *And stand embedded in the English tongue*
> *Till it grow thin, outworn, and cease to be.—*
> *So is't ordained by That Which all ordains ;*
> *For words were never winged with apter grace.*
> *Or blent with happier choice of time and place,*
> *To hold the imagination of this strenuous race.*

To Bonaparte in the final scene in Bossu Wood [2] the Spirit of the Years breathes : " The Will in thee has moved thee," the Will of which he had before declared,[3] "Some force within me, baffling mine intent, harries me onward, whether I will or no." It is the Immanent that urges all, and, it must be noted, not only the seemingly mighty and powerful spirits among men, but also the humble individuals —all are alike tools in the hands of the Great Artificer. As a summary of Hardy's view of the Will as the inherent force underlying all movements, whether of

---

[1] *Dynasts*, I, 5, v.   [2] III, 7, ix.   [3] II, 1, viii.

peoples or individuals, the following passage may be cited—[1]

> *So doth the Will objectify itself*
> *In likeness of a sturdy people's wrath,*
> *Which takes no count of the new trends of time,*
> *Trusting ebbed glory in a present need.—*
> *What if their strength should equal not their fire,*
> *And their devotion dull their vigilance ?—*
> *Uncertainly, by fits, the Will doth work*
> *In Brunswick's blood, their chief, as in themselves ;*
> *It ramifies in streams that intermit*
> *And make their movement vague, old-fashioned, slow*
> *To foil the modern methods counterposed !*

The basic conception of the Immanency of the Will leads Hardy as well as Schopenhauer to a recognition of the unity in historical events, a unity which is designated as a " Plan," although ordinary planning as a result of conscious forethought may not be predicated to the Unconscious Will. All finite intentions, purposes, and cross-purposes of the antagonists are ruled and swayed by the Will " that wills above the will of each, yet is but the will of all conjunctively." [2] The deepest sense and the ultimate significance of the scenes in the British Parliament is the realization that in spite of the blindness, short-sightedness, vanity, unmindfulness of imminent danger, stupid wrangling, and clumsy flattery of professional politicians, the Will proceeds according

---

[1] *Dynasts*, II, i, iii. It is utterly beyond comprehension how readers and self-appointed critics of *The Dynasts* can fail to see the resemblances, not only in thought but in peculiarities of philosophical phraseology, between this and similar passages and the major writings of Schopenhauer, or how scholars of repute can assert, as has been done, that Hardy's " Weltanschauung " is a result of the influence of Bergson, and not of the German metaphysician.

[2] III, i, v.

to its own designs.[1] Likewise the Ironic Spirits
thus satirize the efforts of peace-making bodies—[2]

> *The Congress of Vienna sits*
> *And war becomes a war of wits,*
> *Where every Power perpends withal*
> *Its dues as large, its friends' as small ;*
> *Till Priests of Peace prepare once more*
> *To fight as they have fought before !*

For ironical effects similar to this, the cross-purposes of the antagonists are frequently emphasized.
The proclamations of opposing commanders, pompous
speeches which seem to the Spirits to be but " tongued
afar " by puppets, are set over against each other.
Such are the messages of Villeneuve and Nelson
before Trafalgar[3] and of Napoleon and Alexander
before the Russian campaign.[4] Lauriston and
Villeneuve both declare themselves as eager to shape
their " intentions " to Napoleon's " will," but the
reader must realize, as do the Spirits of the Overworld, that " there is but one Will here."[5] There
is, to the undeluded philosopher, but little difference
between the signification of the gay ballads sung by
the French before the battle, and the religious psalms
intoned by the Russians—the Will is unmindful of
both.[6]

It is evident from this that in Hardy's scheme of
things no reform-movement can possibly inaugurate
any sudden and radical change. " Amid the strange
pranks played by change " the Spirit of the Years
still recognizes " the old Laws, and phase on phase
of men's dynastic and imperial moils shape on accustomed lines."[7] To one who accepts the implications of this and similar observations, the prevalent

---

[1] *Dynasts*, I, 1, iii.   [2] III, 5, i.   [3] I, 5, i.   [4] III, 1, i.
[5] I, 2, ii.   [6] III, 1, iv.   [7] Fore-Scene.

idea that a strong personality can by its inherent force compel the course of history to enter entirely new channels appears ridiculous.

For the benefit of the younger Spirits of the Pities the Will is repeatedly " visualized " to demonstrate the unity of events. This " enlightenment " of the Pities is in reality directed toward the enlightenment of such men as insist on seeing in history the clash of the powers of light and darkness, and the gradual, but inevitable victory of Right over Evil. This popular but, according to Hardy, logically fallacious view is an outgrowth of the belief in a beneficent and anthropomorphically conceived Providence. In spite of its flaws as a philosophy of the universe it is tenaciously adhered to by the strong-willed and heroic Pities. Nevertheless their faith is sorely tried when, during the Battle of Leipzig—

So massive is the contest that we soon fail to individualize combatants as beings, and can only observe them as amorphous drifts, clouds, waves of conscious atoms, surging and rolling together. . . .[1]

All phenomena, animate and inanimate, and all events, however separated in space and time, are viewed but as essential parts of one unified system—

> *What are Space and Time? A fancy!—*
> *Lo, by Vision's necromancy*
> *Muscovy will now unroll;*
> *Where for cork and olive-tree*
> *Shriveling firs and birches be.*
>
> *Though such features lie afar*
> *From events Peninsular,*
> *These, amid their dust and thunder,*
> *Form with those, as scarce asunder,*
> *Parts of one compacted whole.*[2]

[1] *Dynasts*, III, 3, ii.   [2] III, 1, iii.

The whole clash of nations described in *The Dynasts* is thus contemptuously appraised by the Spirit of the Years in the opening of the After-Scene—

> *Thus doth the Great Foresightless mechanize*
> *In blank entrancement now as evermore*
> *Its ceaseless artistries in Circumstance*
> *Of curious stuff and braid, as just foreshown.*
> *   Yet but one flimsy riband of its web*
> *Have we here watched in weaving—web Enorme,*
> *Whose furthest hem and selvage may extend*
> *To where the roars and plashings of the flames*
> *Of earth-invisible suns swell noisily,*
> *And onwards into ghastly gulfs of sky,*
> *Where hideous presences churn through the dark—*
> *Monsters of magnitude without a shape,*
> *Hanging amid deep wells of nothingness.*

A necessary consequence of the assumption of this cosmic viewpoint is the realization of the littleness of men and the futility of all their designs. They are conceived as mere " earthlings," imagining that they influence events, but in reality completely ignorant of the mighty forces that hold sway in the " ghast depths of unlimited space." The race of men is transient and insignificant in a scheme of things that embraces " endless Time." [1] Thus to the receding Intelligences, Milan with all the pomp of its coronation ceremonies, appears but as a minute toy or plaything—

The exterior of the Cathedral takes the place of the interior, and the point of view recedes, the whole fabric smalling into distance and becoming like a rare, delicately carved alabaster ornament. The city itself sinks to miniature, the Alps show afar as a white corrugation. . . . [2]

The march of an army is like the movement of mollusks on a leaf,[3] or like the silent insect-creep.[4]

[1] *Dynasts*, III, 1, iii.   [2] I, 3, i.   [3] I, 3, ii.   [4] I, 3, ii.

Soldiers digging trenches appear as "innumerable human figures busying themselves as cheese-mites," [1] and heroes like Napoleon are "like meanest insects on obscurest leaves, but incidents and tools of Earth's unfolding." [2] The pompous speeches of great men "die away to ripples," [3] and their sufferings and death-agonies, so pitiful and horrible to human view, are quite insignificant in an "unmindful" scheme of things.[4] Corpses covered over with snow are merely "pimples by the roadside." In short, "nothing" that men do "matters much." [5]

Throughout *The Dynasts* there is emphasized the Schopenhauerian doctrine that while history unfolds before our eyes the spectacle of uninterrupted change and teaches us that at all times there was something different, philosophy maintains that this change is non-essential and that at all times there was the same. The whole epic-drama is but an illustration of the statement of the Spirit of the Years in the Fore-Scene—

> But old laws operate yet ; and phase and phase
> Of men's dynastic and imperial moils
> Shape on accustomed lines.

History is an unbroken, uniform, and unchanging concatenation of events bound together by the mysterious workings of the Immanent Will.

Another principle of Schopenhauer is adhered to by Hardy in his treatment of historical events : the attempt at depth of perception rather than breadth of description, and the portrayal of the smallest incident as a true mirror of the government of the universe. What is the whole picture unfolded in

---

[1] *Dynasts*, II, 6, i.   [2] III, 7, ix.   [3] I, 1, v.
[4] III, 1, ix.   [5] III, 5, iv.

the poems and in *The Dynasts* but that which Schopenhauer finds in every phase of human life, " die Trefflichkeit, Tugend, ja Heiligkeit Einzelner, die Verkehrtheit, Erbärmlichkeit und Tuecke der Meisten, die Ruchlosigkeit Mancher." [1]   The scene in *The Dynasts* which makes the most immediate and the most lasting effect on the casual reader is not one of the court- or battle-scenes, but a picture of the meanest and obscurest dregs and scum of the British army in a miserable and filthy cellar in Spain.[2] Schopenhauer's observation that the history of a village in all essentials is identical to the history of a kingdom is again wonderfully illustrated in many of Hardy's novels, in which a whole philosophy of life is unfolded by a story laid in

one of those sequestered spots outside the gates of the world where may usually be found more meditation than action, and more passivity than meditation ; yet where, from time to time, no less than in other places, dramas of a grandeur and unity truly Sophoclean are enacted in the real. . . . [3]

Of *Two on a Tower* Hardy writes—

This slightly built romance was the outcome of a wish to set the emotional history of two infinitesimal lives against the stupendous background of the universe, and to impart to the reader the sentiment that of these contrasting magnitudes the smaller might be the greater to them as men. . . . [4]

The view of universal history which regards the smallest event in the everyday life of the obscurest individual as important as the mighty upheavals that receive the lion's share of the chronicler's attentions, is also found expressed in such a poem as *The Roman Gravemounds* (*SC*), in which the poet observes a man,

[1] Sch. i, 327.
[2] *Dynasts*, II, 3, i.
[3] *The Woodlanders*, chap. i.
[4] Preface (1895) to *Two on a Tower*.

oblivious of the remains of the ancient grandeur that
was Rome, burying his dead kitten among the relics
of the once magnificent Empire, and saying—

> " Here say you that Cæsar's warriors lie ?—
> But my little white cat was my only friend !
> Could she but live, might the record die
> Of Cæsar, his legions, his aims, his end ! "
>
> Well, Rome's long rule is oft and again
> A theme for the sages of history,
> And the small furred life was worth no one's pen ;
> Yet its mourner's mood has a charm for me.

Hardy's definitive statement of the intellectual
grounds upon which he bases his own Monistic
attitude is to be found in the notable Preface to
The Dynasts, in which he explains and defends the
introduction of his celestial machinery to represent
and expound his theory of the Will—

The wide prevalence of the Monistic theory of the Universe
forbade, in this twentieth century, the importation of Divine
personages from any antique Mythology as ready-made sources
or channels of Causation, even in verse, and excluded the
celestial machinery of, say, *Paradise Lost,* as peremptorily as
that of the *Iliad* or the *Eddas.* And the abandonment of the
masculine pronoun in allusions to the First or Fundamental
Energy seemed a necessary and logical consequence of the
long abandonment by thinkers of the anthropomorphic conception of the same.

It will be observed that, as with Schopenhauer, the
conception of an external, supramundane First Cause
or Deity is ruled out of account by Hardy at the
very start. He very rarely uses the term First Cause,
and never in the traditional sense, but prefers " Fundamental inherent Energy." Again, although he gives
unreserved assent to the Monistic theory of the
Universe, as opposed to religious Dualism, he is

emphatically not a materialistic monist, but an ideal-
ist, as has been demonstrated in the preceding chapter.
It is of some significance that, before the display of
the anatomy of the Will at Austerlitz,[1] he uses as
a synonym for the Immanent, the term "world-
Soul," an expression germane to Pantheism.

Like every serious man, Hardy shows at all times
an intense interest in religion. One can easily
observe how his interest manifests itself in the
many echoes of the Bible in nearly all his books.
The Respectable Burgher on the Higher Criticism (PP) is
a rather long-drawn-out sneer at those sceptics who
make it their business to strip the Bible of all its
old-time glamour. At the same time he shows an
undeniable interest in the true history of religion as
it has been presented by those who have examined
the Scriptural texts with both critical and reverent
care. In *God's Funeral (SC)* he speaks of the man-
projected figure of God as having been framed jealous
and fierce at first, and endowed with the divine attributes of justice and mercy in the course of time.
This is a rough summary of the results of Higher
Criticism.

With regard to his own position on the subject,
however, we find that he is again in essential harmony
with Schopenhauer : the conception of the Immanent
Will leads inevitably to a denial of the traditional
claim of religion as a system of divinely revealed
truth. Hardy is not an implacable and inveterate
enemy of religion, but is in sympathy with some of
its ideals, and frequently acknowledges its value, even
while he recognizes the sham and hypocrisy of certain
of its confessors. The real sincerity of his agnosticism
is feelingly presented in *The Impercipient (WP)*. At

[1] *Dynasts*, I, 6, iii.

a Cathedral service the poet bewails the fact that his sincerity has made him an outcast from " this bright believing band " ; that he somehow can find no comfort in the " All's well " with which believers console themselves ; and he asks—

> O, doth a bird deprived of wings
> Go earthbound wilfully !

He cannot reconcile the idea of an omnipotent and merciful Deity with the human sufferings that he witnesses daily : in *God-Forgotten* (*PP*) he imagines that as soon as the attention of the Supreme Being is called to the plight of the world, all evils and wretchedness will be mended.[1] Some such mystery as that of the fourth dimension must reside " within the ethic of God's will." [2] Elsewhere God is conceived as the unconscious, non-ethical creator of conscious, " moral," and suffering humanity.[3] Man is accused of being himself the manufacturer of this unnecessary, external, and unmoral Deity, who is now dying as the ancient creeds lose their prestige.[4] Hardy's conception of an unconscious, if beneficent, God imperceptibly merges into his view of all phenomena as manifestations of the Will. In such a comparatively early poem as *Nature's Questioning* (*WP*) the children of Nature ask—

> Has some vast Imbecility [5]
> Mighty to build and blend,
> But impotent to tend,
> Framed us in jest, and left us now to hazardry ?

[1] The same idea can be found in *The Bedridden Peasant to an Unknowing God* (*PP*), and in *By the Earth's Corpse* (*PP*). See also *God's Education*, in *Time's Laughingstocks* (hereafter abbreviated *TL*).
[2] *A Dream-Question* (*TL*).
[3] *New-Year's Eve* (*TL*).
[4] See *A Plaint to Man* (*SC*), and *God's Funeral* (*SC*).
[5] Cf. Nietzsche, *Also Sprach Zarathustra* (Von Hinterweltlern).

" Or come we of an Automaton
    Unconscious of our pains ? . . .
    Or are we live remains
Of Godhead dying downwards, brain and eye now gone ?

Or is it that some high Plan betides,
    As yet not understood
    Of Evil stormed by Good,
We the forlorn hope over which Achievement strides ? "

The title of the above poem, as well as the later lyric *He Wonders About Himself* (*MV*) shows Hardy again in sympathy with Schopenhauer in his recognition of the fact that religious thought originated in an innate metaphysical need of man who wonders at his own existence and who seeks relief from the bewilderment with which he must needs face the problem of his place in the Cosmos.

He likewise recognizes in religion Schopenhauer's " metaphysics of the masses " : he observes its consolatory value as an escape from reality and the distresses of the world of phenomena. His disagreement with it as a harmonious and logical explanation or interpretation of reality does not prevent him from appreciating its " renunciative " excellencies. This can be clearly observed in such a poem as *On a Fine Morning* (*PP*).

Whence comes Solace ?—Not from seeing
What is doing, suffering, being,
Not from noting Life's conditions,
Not from heeding Time's monitions ;
    But in cleaving to the Dream,
    And in gazing at the gleam
    Whereby gray things golden seem.

Thus do I this heyday, holding
Shadows but as lights unfolding,

" *What of the Immanent Will?* "

As no specious show this moment
With its iris-hued embowment ;
    But as nothing other than
    Part of a benignant plan ;
Proof that earth was made for man.

There are no allusions in Hardy to the non-christian religions from which Schopenhauer drew so much inspiration, nor does he ever condemn Judaism as Schopenhauer does. It is a peculiar thing that no Jews appear among all his characters. The symbol of the " Wheel," so often encountered in *The Dynasts*, however, may have been employed with some realization of its Hindu-origin. Sometimes it is possible also to discover in the lyric poems strong hints of a distinctly pagan Venus-worship, as in *The Well-Beloved* (*PP*), but in *Aquæ Sulis* (*SC*), which can be compared to Swinburne's *Hymn to Proserpina*, the poet finds both the Pagan and the Christian creeds equally outworn.

Naturally the claims of Christianity as a world-religion in the strictest sense of the term, explaining the mysteries of the whole universe of unlimited space in endless time, seem preposterous to him. Even though he has nothing but admiration for its uncorrupted pristine character of holiness and love, it is to him merely

A local cult, called Christianity,
Which the wild dramas of the wheeling spheres
Include, with divers others such, in dim
Pathetical and brief parentheses,
Beyond whose span, uninfluenced, unconcerned,
The systems of the suns go sweeping on
With all their many-mortaled planet train
In mathematic roll unceasingly.[1]

[1] *Dynasts*, I, i, vi.

The unwarrantable expansion of a simple gospel into an elaborate ecclesiastical system of doctrine and ritual finds little favour in his eyes. There is a touch of disdain in the Pities' question, " What is the creed that these rich rites disclose ? " in the coronation scene in Milan. At the sight of the bulbous church-tops of Moscow Davout exclaims, " Souls must be rotten in this region to need so much repairing." Belief in miracles is as superstitious to Hardy as the worship of relics. He as well as Napoleon sneers at the Russians who kneel in front of their icons and other religious insignia before the Battle of Borodino.[1] Nevertheless, Bonaparte harbours the superstitious belief that he is ruled by the star of Destiny, and that " God has given him the crown," [2] and the English King's belief in " Heaven's confidence in him and his line " calls forth a biting sarcastic comment.[3]

Hardy's disbelief in a Higher Power endowed with a personality leads him occasionally to an indulgence in outspoken satire, as in *Royal Sponsors (MV)*, where the sacrament of baptism is profaned by professed Christians out of deference to the hollow magnificence of temporal pomp. The representatives of Christianity, priests and clergymen, are singled out particularly for ironical comment, although it must be noted that Hardy is much more liberal, sympathetic, and fair in his attitude toward the clergy than is Schopenhauer. He never doubts their sincerity—only he is vexed and saddened that they occasionally doubt his. In the novels many of the most admirable figures are the parsons, such as Mr. Raunham in *Desperate Remedies*, old Mr. Clare in *Tess*, and the Bishop of Melchester in *Two on a Tower*, who

---

[1] *Dynasts*, III, 1, iv.   [2] I, 1, vi.   [3] I, 4, 1.

is, in the author's own words, " every inch a gentle-man." [1] Hardy's ministers usually prove to be forces for good in the stories in which they play their parts. The " curate's kindness " in the poem of that name [2] proves to have been ill-advised, but it was none the less well-meant. Nevertheless, his eyes are not closed to the patent insincerity and shameful hypocrisy of many of the " self-styled ser-vants of the Highest." Much of the misery that overtakes the unfortunate characters in *A Pair of Blue Eyes* can be traced directly to the conceit, bigotry, stupidity, and narrow-minded egoism of Mr. Swancourt in that romance. To the sharp and clever exposé of the preacher's hypocrisy in that " Satire of Circumstance," *In Church,* one need only add the figure of the shrewd and unscrupulous church dignitary, Cardinal Archbishop Caprara, who plays alike with his religion and with the Emperor at Milan.[3]

Hardy recognizes in religion a positive influence for evil when its true nature and purposes are mis-understood : *The Church-Builder (PP)* is a tragedy of the terrible consequences of faith and devotion carried to extremes by a too ardent enthusiast. He realizes that religious feeling can be and has been abused in order to arouse hatred and fanaticism—that it then intensifies the cruel and destructive instincts in man and makes wars more horrible. At such times he is in accord with Schopenhauer's favourite proverb : " Hinter dem Kreuze steht der Teufel."

We have noticed that Schopenhauer condemns the Jewish and Christian religions because their doctrines of man's exclusive right to the possession of an im-

---

[1] See the Preface.   [2] Sub-titled " A Workhouse-Irony."
[3] *Dynasts,* I, i, vi.

mortal soul has led them to the most despicable inhumanity to animals, creatures in reality no lower than man, since all are on the same level as mere objectifications of the Immanent Will. No reader of Hardy can have failed to notice the complete agreement with this view presented in the novels, poems, and *Dynasts*, although Hardy does not trouble himself about the metaphysical basis upon which Schopenhauer founds or interprets his humanitarianism. The dog who helps poor forsaken Fanny Robin in *Far from the Madding Crowd* [1] is one of the very noblest of all the figures of English fiction, a " personification of night in its sad, solemn, and benevolent character "—and this " ideal embodiment of canine greatness " is stoned away after his act of heroic devotion. Or take this passage from *The Return of the Native*—[2]

A bustard haunted the spot, and not many years before this five and twenty might have been seen in Egdon at one time. Marsh-harriers looked up from the valley by Wildeve's. A cream-coloured courser had used to visit this hill, a bird so rare that not more than a dozen have ever been seen in England ; but a barbarian rested neither night nor day till he had shot the African truant, and after that event cream-coloured coursers thought fit to enter Egdon no more.

In *Tess* [3] there is an even more passionate denunciation of the practice of murdering birds, accompanied by a picture of such pathos and horror that even the misery of the heroine is momentarily forgotten. Of the perpetrators we read—

She had occasionally caught glimpses of these men in girl-hood, looking over hedges or peeping through bushes, and pointing their guns, strangely accoutred, a bloodthirsty light in their eyes. She had been told that, rough and brutal as they seemed just then, they were not like this all the year round, but were, in fact, quite civil persons, save during certain weeks of autumn and winter, when, like the inhabitants of the Malay Peninsula, they ran amuck, and made it their purpose to destroy life—in this case harmless feathered creatures brought into being by artificial means solely to gratify the propensity, at once so unmannerly and so unchivalrous towards their weaker fellows in Nature's teeming family.

Jude is full of similar illustrations. The hero himself is a humanitarian like Tess, and allows his sensitivity and generosity towards the rooks to get him into trouble with Farmer Trontham at the very outset of his career.[1] He is a boy " who could not bear to hunt anything. He never brought home a nest of young birds without lying awake in misery half the night after. . . . He could scarcely bear to see trees cut down or lopped, from a fancy that it hurt them. . . . He carefully picked his way on tiptoe among the earthworms without killing a single one." The notorious pig-killing scene[2] must also be mentioned, in which, among other things, " the white snow, stained with the blood of his fellow-mortal, wore an illogical look to him as a lover of justice, not to say a Christian. . . ." The rabbit entrapped in the cruel gin,[3] the sale of Sue's pet pigeons,[4] and the horse kicked in the belly at the gates of " a college in the most religious and educational city in the world," [5] give opportunity for equally effective propaganda.

The same passionate pity for helpless creatures is expressed in *The Blind Bird* (*MV*) already quoted, in many an early villanelle and triolet,[6] and in that

[1] Part I, chap. ii.   [2] Part I, chap. x.   [3] Part IV, chap. ii.
[4] Part V, chap. vi.   [5] Part VI, chap. i.
[6] *The Caged Freed and Home Again* (*PP*), *Birds at Winter Nightfall* (*PP*), and *The Puzzled Game-Birds* (*PP*). See also *The Caged Goldfinch* (*MV*).

masterpiece, *The Darkling Thrush* (*PP*), in which the aged bird, " frail, gaunt, and small, in blast-beruffled plume," flings his soul upon the growing gloom as if aware of a blessed Hope of which the poet is unconscious.   There is delicious satire in *Wagtail and Baby* (*TL*)—

> A baby watched a ford, whereto
>   A wagtail came for drinking ;
> A blaring bull went wading through,
>   The wagtail showed no shrinking.
>
> A stallion splashed his way across,
>   The birdie nearly sinking ;
> He gave his plumes a twitch and toss,
>   And held his own unblinking.
>
> Next saw the baby round the spot
>   A mongrel slowly slinking ;
> The wagtail gazed, but faltered not
>   In dip and sip and prinking.
>
> A perfect gentleman then neared ;
>   The wagtail, in a winking,
> With terror rose and disappeared ;
>   The baby fell a-thinking.

Here " only man is vile."

The Dynasts likewise contains many expressions of pity for animals as war-sufferers.   After the Battle of Borodino, the Spirit of the Pities observes—

> *Those shady shapes*
> *Are horses, maimed in myriads, tearing round*
> *In maddening pangs, the harnessings they wear*
> *Clanking discordant jingles as they tear !* [1]

At the Battle of Wagram " docile horses roll to dismal death and horrid mutilation,"[2] on the return

---

[1] *Dynasts*, III, 1, v.   Note also II, 2, vii.   [2] II, 4, v.

from Moscow " the worn and harassed horses slumber as they walk," [1] and the only sound heard on that frightful march was " the flogging of the wind-broken and lacerated horses." [2]   Finally, the Chorus of the Years thus describes the effects of the Battle of Waterloo—[3]

> *Yea, the coneys scared by the thud of hoofs,*
> *And their white scuts flash at their vanishing heels,*
> *And swallows abandon the hamlet roofs.*
>
> *The mole's tunnelled chambers are crushed by wheels,*
> *The lark's eggs scattered, their owners fled ;*
> *And the hedgehog's household the sapper unseals.*
>
> *The snail draws in at the terrible tread,*
> *But in vain ; he is crushed by the felloe-rim ;*
> *The worm asks what can be overhead,*
>
> *And wriggles deep from a scene so grim,*
> *And guesses him safe ; for he does not know*
> *What a foul red flood will be soaking him !*
>
> *Beaten about by the heel and toe*
> *Are butterflies, sick of the day's long rheum,*
> *To die of a worse than the weather-foe.*
>
> *Trodden and bruised to a miry tomb*
> *Are ears that have greened but will never be gold,*
> *And flowers in the bud that will never bloom.*

[1] *Dynasts*, III, 3, iii.   [2] III, 1, 7.   [3] III, 6, viii.

CHAPTER FOUR

" EARTH'S JACKACLOCKS "

THE IMMEDIATE consciousness of every man finds deeply rooted within itself the conviction of perfect freedom of action ; superficial reflective thought and the employment of the most rudimentary principles of logical conclusion at once leads to the complete denial of all freedom and a fatalistic belief in destiny ; it is the province of the philosopher to harmonize the two contrasting views and to demonstrate the essential unity of what has been termed free-will and necessity.

That the Will is free, Schopenhauer says, follows from the fact that it is the thing-in-itself. As the thing-in-itself the Will does not lie within the sphere of perception, is in no sense an object, and cannot be subordinate to the principle of sufficient reason. It is groundless and causeless, the universal cause of every phenomenon, yet itself neither the effect of any cause nor the consequent of any reason. It is not only free but autonomous in the highest sense of the term. The phenomenon, on the other hand, we recognize as absolutely subjected to the principle of sufficient reason, and as " necessity " is identical with " following from given grounds," all that belongs to the phenomenon, that is, the whole objective world, is determined with necessity and can in no respect be otherwise than it is. However, as the essential nature of every phenomenon is Will, it shares in this respect the freedom of the Autonomous Will.[1]

Here, then, Schopenhauer finds the essential unity of freedom and necessity. It is a mistake to speak of absolute necessity ; for the necessity of an event is always conditional upon its cause : only in its relation to this cause it is necessary, but with reference to everything else it is casual and a matter of chance. Neither is there any absolute chance. For even its queerest pranks will with advancing knowledge be recognized as necessary effects of a given cause, links in the chain of cause and effect, and only with reference to things which are not their cause do they bear the character of the casual. Necessity and chance, then, spring from one and the same root and are the two sides of one and the same thing.[2]

As the Autonomous Will in the sphere of nature determines the course of events through the operation of irresistible causes, so in the sphere of human life it determines the course of action through the operation of irresistible motives. Schopenhauer's attempt at the solution of the age-long problem may be summed up in one sentence : Man always does what he wants to do ; but he must want to do what he wants, because he is what he is. Every action is the necessary result of the combination of character and motive. As the whole tree is only the constantly repeated manifestation of one and the same tendency which exhibits itself in its simplest form in the fibre, and recurs and is easily recognized in the construction of

---

[1] Sch. i, 375 sqq. Cf. i, 180 ; i, 226 ; *Die beiden Grundprobleme der Ethik*, 383 sqq.

[2] Sch., *Parerga* i, 238 : " Die im tiefsten Grunde der Dinge liegende Einheit des Notwendigen und Zufälligen " ; 241 : " Einheit der tiefliegenden Wurzel der Notwendigkeit und Zufälligkeit." Cf. i, 591.

the leaf, the shoot, the branch, and the trunk, so all deeds of a man are merely the constantly repeated expressions of his intelligible character, in the Kantian sense, and the sum of these expressions forms his empirical character.[1] To doubt the unavoidable necessity of an action resulting from the operation of a certain motive upon a certain character—provided that the motive is known and understood ; for not the motive present, but the motive known and understood incites action [2]—is as unreasonable as to question the fact that the three angles of any triangle are together equal to two right angles.

The universal illusion of freedom of action springs, according to Schopenhauer, chiefly from the fact that the causeless nature of the Autonomous Will manifests itself most clearly in the will of man and is here directly and immediately known in self-consciousness. Then again, the apparent difference in the action of a man under apparently identical circumstances has given rise to the impression that he is the possessor of a *liberum arbitrium indifferentiæ*. In reality the difference in action is caused by the difference in circumstances. On the first occasion he may not understand the motive as clearly as he does on the second. In each case the motive—as far as it is a real motive, that is : known and understood—calls forth from his character the action with necessity.[3]

To elucidate this thought Schopenhauer employs the following illustration—

We will imagine a man standing in the street and saying to himself : " It is six o'clock in the evening ; the day's

---

[1] Sch. i, 378.

[2] As the Scholastics used to say : *Causa finalis movet non secundum suum esse reale, sed secundum esse cognitum.*

[3] Sch. i, 384.

work is done. I can now take a walk ; or I can go into
my club ; or I can climb upon the tower to watch the sunset ;
I can also go to the theatre ; I can also visit this or that
friend ; yes, I can run out of the city into the wide world
and never return. All this is completely in my power, I
have perfect freedom to choose what I please ; however, I
do nothing of the kind, but just as voluntarily go home to
my wife." That is just as if the water said : " I can rise in
mounting waves (yes ! namely in the ocean during a storm),
I can foamingly fall down into the depth (yes ! in the cataract),
I can as a free column rise into the air (yes ! in the foun-
tain), I can even evaporize and completely disappear (yes ! at a
heat of 80 degrees) ; but just at present I do nothing of all
this but remain voluntarily quiet and clear in the smooth
pond." As the water can do all those things only when the
determining causes arise, so the man mentioned above can do
what he imagines to be able to do only on condition that the
necessary motives are presented. Being what he is, he can
under certain circumstances do only one thing, and that he
must do with necessity. . . . I can do what I will : I can,
if I will, give all to the poor and thereby myself become a
pauper,—yes, if I will !—But I am not able to will it, because
the opposing motives dominate me so strongly as to make it
impossible for me to will it. But if I had a different character,
to the extent that I were a saint, then I could will it. However, in that case I could not help willing it, and would do it
of necessity.[1]

As the action of man is irresistibly determined by
his character and the motives operating upon it, no
real change is possible for him, and nothing of what
theologians have termed conversion or regeneration
has any place in the system of Schopenhauer. He
admits that the action of a man may undergo notice-
able changes, for its form depends upon the degree
of clearness with which the intellect apprehends the
motive presented. But the character itself remains
unalterably the same, he can only do what he wills,

[1] Sch., *Freiheit des Willens*, p. 421 sqq.

and *velle non discitur*. The same character may express itself in a hundred different lives ; but these differences are only the different forms of the same thing, and the essentials always remain. Thus, for example, it is immaterial whether a man plays for nuts or for crowns ; but whether a man cheats or plays fairly, that is the essential thing.[1] If a man becomes firmly convinced that every good action will be repaid him a hundredfold in a future life, such a conviction affects him in precisely the same way as a good bill of exchange at a very long date, and he can give alms from mere egoism as from another point of view he would steal from egoism. The great influence of knowledge upon action is to be recognized, but the essential nature and character is unchangeable. The character may show itself differently at every period of life, an impetuous and wild youth may be succeeded by a staid and sober and manly age, and passions to which a man gave way in his youth may afterwards be voluntarily restrained. This, however, implies in no way a change of character, but is simply caused by a fuller understanding of the motive. Especially what is bad in a character will come out more strongly with time ; the first evil deed is the guaranty of innumerable similar ones, and in spite of all his resolutions and reflections he must from the beginning of his life to the end carry out the very character which he himself condemns and play his part to the end.

From these premises the futility of all remorse becomes apparent. Discontent with himself, Schopenhauer says, is indeed the severest pain that can come to man. Yet remorse is only an indication of improved knowledge, and never a symptom of a

[1] Sch. i, 221 ; cf. 385.

changed will. Man can never regret what he has
willed, but only what he has done ; for completer
knowledge may teach him that he was led by false
conceptions, and committed deeds that were not in
conformity with his essential nature. Thus remorse
springs not from a change of will, but from a change
of knowledge.

One does not have to seek very far in the writings
of Thomas Hardy for evidence of his complete agreement with the deterministic theory outlined above.
First of all, he fully shares Schopenhauer's view as to
the essential unity of chance and necessity. In *The
Dynasts*, the English King's spurning of Bonaparte's
peace-overtures seems to occur out of pure chance,
caprice, and arbitrariness, whereupon the Spirit of
the Pities speculates upon the possible result of a
different action under the circumstances—

> *Ill chanced it that the English monarch George
> Did not respond to the said emperor !* [1]

The Spirit Sinister, however, " sees good sport
therein," realizing that through motives of dynastic
pride, prejudice, and others unknown alike to himself and to other men, the king was swayed to do as
he did by the Will. A necessary action decreed by
the Autonomous Will appeared to men as blind
chance.

A series of seemingly chance happenings frustrates
Napoleon's cherished plan for the invasion of Britain.
Admiral Decres thus reports the disastrous course of
events—

> Sire, at the very juncture when the fleets
> Sailed out from Ferrol, fever raged aboard
> *L'Achille* and *L'Algeciras* : later on,
> Mischief assailed our Spanish comrades' ships ;

[1] *Dynasts*, I, i, i.

Several ran foul of neighbours ; whose new hurts,
Being added to their innate clumsiness,
Gave hap the upper hand ; and in quick course
Demoralized the whole ; until Villeneuve,
Judging that Calder now with Nelson rode,
And prescient of unparallelled disaster
If he pushed on in so disjoint a trim,
Bowed to the inevitable ; and thus perforce,
Leaving to other opportunity
Brest and the Channel scheme, with vast regret
Steered southbound into Cadiz.[1]

This passage is particularly significant because Villeneuve is reported in it to have realized that " hap "
had the upper hand, and so to have bowed to the
" inevitable," thus feeling the essential unity of
chance and necessity. The mishaps to the French
and Spanish fleets appear to human observers as
things that might not have been, yet they were in
reality links in a long chain of events foreordained
by the Will in its greater scheme, of which the frus-
tration of Napoleon's naval venture was a part.

Napoleon recognizes clearly the " oneness of the
deeply hidden root from which both necessity and
chance spring," when he offers to the defeated
General Mack this bit of consolation—

War, General, ever has its ups and downs,
And you must take the better and the worse
As impish chance or destiny ordains.[2]

The chance location of the British Isles, isolated from
the Continent, is seen by Hardy to have necessitated
their development as a sea-power that would eventually prove to be the pivotal force in the great clash
of nations. As the Ironic Spirits express it—

But the *Weaving Will from eternity,*
Hemming them in by a circling sea
Evolved the fleet of the Englishry.[3]

[1] *Dynasts,* I, 3, i.   [2] I, 4, v.   [3] II, 1, vi.

The death of Pitt at the critical moment when he had devised plans for " Europe's reason-wrought repose " appeared as blind chance ; yet it had to occur to remove an obstacle to the unhindered course of the destiny-decreed Historical Calamity.[1] The matrimonial career of Napoleon appears as a strange interweaving of chance and necessity : the sterility of Josephine, the slighting of Alexander's sister, the marriage with Marie Louise, apparently chance happenings, unpremeditated and hastily performed, prove to have been inevitable events to bring about a foreordained end. When the Conqueror sees the Queen of Prussia, he meditates—

> Had she come sooner with those sweet, beseeching eyes of hers, who knows what might not have happened ! But she didn't come sooner, and I have kept in my right mind.[2]

Again, when news of the death of the unhappy lady reaches Alexander, he remembers—

> Strangely, the present English Prince of Wales
> Was wished to husband her. Had wishes won,
> They might have varied Europe's history.[3]

The absolute dominance of the Autonomous Will is brought home to the reader of *The Dynasts* by a number of highly suggestive images and epithets employed with a view of destroying every illusion of the freedom of human action. The Will is " the Prime Mover of the Gear " and the " Director of the puppet-show." To correct the illogical sympathies of the Pities the Spirit of the Years bids the Intelligences

> . . . *watch the spectacle of Europe's moves*
> *In her embroil, as they were self-ordained*
> *According to the naïve and liberal creed*
> *Of our great-hearted young Compassionates,*

[1] *Dynasts*, II, 1, ii.   [2] II, 1, viii.   [3] II, 5, vii.

> *Forgetting the Prime Mover of the gear,*
> *As puppet-watchers him who pulls the strings.——*
> *You'll mark the twitchings of this Bonaparte*
> *As he with other figures foots his reel,*
> *Until he twitch him into his lonely grave :*
> *Also regard the frail ones that his flings*
> *Have made gyrate like animalcula*
> *In tepid pools. .*   [1]

At its first visualization the Will is described by the Pities as a many-coiled monster——

> *Strange waves I sight, like winds grown visible,*
> *Which bear men's forms on their innumerable coils,*
> *Twining and serpentining round and through.*
> *Also retracting threads like gossamers——*
> *Except in being irresistible——*
> *Which complicate with some, and balance all.* [2]

Again it is viewed as the arm or the body, free in itself, that moves mortals like its own fingers——

> *So the Will heaves through space and moulds the times*
> *With mortals for Its fingers !   We shall see*
> *Again men's passions, virtues, visions, crimes,*
> > *Obey resistlessly*
> *The purposive, unmotived, dominant Thing*
> *Which sways in brooding dark their wayfaring.* [3]

At the close of the gruesome picture of the dying English army at Walcheren, the Will is remarkably presented as the Cosmic Organ-player by the Spirit of the Years, who thus chides the Pities for chanting the woes of the fever-stricken host——

> *Why must ye echo as mechanic mimes*
> *These mortal minions' bootless cadences,*
> *Played on the stops of their anatomy*
> *As is the mewling music on the strings*
> *Of yonder ship-masts by the unweeting wind,*

[1] *Dynasts*, Fore-Scene.   [2] Fore-Scene.   [3] II, 4, viii.

" Earth's Jackaclocks "

Or the frail tune upon this withering sedge
That holds its papery blades against the gale ? [1]

As the " Turner of the Wheel " the Will " turns
the handle of this idle show," controlling the waves
of the sea and the swayings of the mountain forests
as well as determining the final end of all supposedly
man-conceived " regal puppet-shows." [2] It is the
Great Necessitator, the Eternal Urger,[3] the High
Influence that sways the English realm with all its
homuncules,[4] the Master-Hand that plays the game
alone,[5] the Back of Things that " hauls the halyards
of the world." [6] And the practical lesson brought
home by this polychromatic imagery is expressed by
the Spirit of the Years—

You cannot swerve the pulsion of the Byss ! [7]

The unhappy lot of man in a scheme of things
ruled by an Autonomous Will whose workings
appear as freakish pranks of chance and time is a
theme that can be found in almost anything that
Hardy has written since his discovery of its wonderful and unlimited possibilities of drama and irony in
A Pair of Blue Eyes. It is the subject of the very
first poem in *Wessex Poems*,[8] as well as one of the last
in *Moments of Vision.*[9] The fatalistic outlook upon
life is immeasurably strengthened in the poems by
Hardy's knowledge and use of the principles of
heredity. In *The Pedigree*, for instance, the poet,
viewing as in a mirror " the long perspective " of his
" begetters, dwindling backward each past each, all
with the family look," begins to

---

[1] *Dynasts*, II, 6, vii. [2] Fore-Scene and After-Scene.
[3] I, 6, iii [4] I, 1, iii. [5] II, 2, iv. [6] III, 7, vii.
[7] Fore-Scene. [8] *The Temporary the All.* [9] *Before Knowledge.*

... divine
That every heave and move and coil I made
Within my brain, and in my mood and speech
     Was in the glass portrayed
As long forestalled by their so making it ;
The first of them, the primest fuglemen of my line,
Being fogged in far antiqueness past surmise and reason's reach.

     Said I then, sunk in tone,
" I am mere continuator and counterfeit !—
     Though thinking, I am I,
And what I do I do myself alone."

Even more strikingly the same idea is expressed in
Heredity (*MV*)—

I am the family face ;
Flesh perishes, I live on,
Projecting trait and trace
Through time and times anon,
And leaping from place to place
Over oblivion.

The years-heired creatures that can
In curve and voice and eye
Despise the human span
Of durance—that is I ;
The eternal thing in man
That heeds no call to die.

To indicate the essential futility of the purposes
and doings of individual men in the Will-determined
universe Hardy has suggested [1] that the actors who
take the parts of the human dramatis personæ deliver
their speeches monotonously, " with dreamy conventional gestures, something in the manner traditionally
maintained by the Christmas mummers, the curiously
hypnotizing impressiveness of whose automatic style
—that of persons who spoke by no will of their own

[1] *Dynasts*, Preface.

—may be remembered by all who have ever experienced it." In the stage-directions to the very first scene we learn that the voices of the Wessex people after the chanting of the Intelligences " sound small and commonplace, as from another medium." The mighty men of the earth, and the chief actors in the historical drama are

> *These flesh-hinged mannikins Its Hands upwind*
> *To click-clack off Its preadjusted laws.*[1]

They are likened to the unsubstantial figures shown on a screen through lantern-slides Of Napoleon the Spirit of the Years says—

> *So let him speak, the while we clearly sight him*
> *Moved like a figure on a lantern-slide.*
> *Which, much amazing uninitiate eyes,*
> *The all-compelling crystal pane but drags*
> *Whither the showman wills.*[2]

Napoleon throughout is viewed as a helpless puppet and an impotent tool in the hands of the Great Artificer. When the Spirit of the Pities becomes exasperated at his inconsistencies, the Spirit of the Years answers—

> *Thou reasonest ever thuswise—even as if*
> *A self-formed force had urged his loud career.*[3]

In the same scene the Spirit of the Years rebukes the Pities for attempting to influence Napoleon and revive the spirit of liberty in his soul, by reminding the " officious sprite " that the Emperor's acts " do but outshape its governings." When the Pities cannot understand how Napoleon can undertake the Russian campaign, the Years produces the vizualiza-

[1] *Dynasts,* Fore-Scene. [2] I, 4, v. [3] I, i, vi.

tion of the Will by which the insignificance of all the human actors is shown. Men such as Bonaparte are in the hands of the Supreme Power but

> *. . . as a brazen rod that stirs the fire*
> *Because it must.*[1]

Napoleon himself recognizes the helplessness of other mortals but, naturally enough, reserves for himself a more important rôle. As he casts off the hapless Josephine, he exclaims—

> What's one woman's future more or less
> Beside the scheme of kings !

little realizing that the future of one emperor or one dynasty more or less is just as insignificant in the vast scheme of the Will.

As helpless as the chief actors in the drama of history are the innocent nations whose sufferings seem to be brought about by the pride, obstinacy, and stupidity of their rulers. In reality it is the Will that entraps them, as it does everything else, like fishes in a net. They cannot slip the " toils they are madding to enmesh us in." [2] Distressed by events which they did not cause, the peoples are " seen writhing, crawling, heaving, and vibrating in their various cities and nationalities." [3] They are but as ninepins to " these bowling hands " of dynasts, and the dynasts themselves are no more.[4] The heart-breaking spectacle of the retreat of the Grand Army is thus explained—

> *The host has turned from Moscow where it lay*
> *And Israel-like, moved by some master-sway*
> *Is made to wander on and waste away.*[5]

[1] *Dynasts*, III, 7, ix.   [2] Fore-Scene.   [3] II, 1, ii.
[4] III, 3, 1.   [5] III, 1, ix.

The same absolute Will that sways men and
nations according to its inscrutable purposes dominates the Spiritual Intelligences with equal tyranny.
The grim boast of the Spirit Sinister about " his
pestilence, fires, famines, and other comedies " are
checked by the Spirit of the Years, " Thinking thou
willst thou dost but indicate." [1]   The elder Phantom
also defends his conduct in inflicting seemingly need-
less mental tortures upon the luckless Villeneuve by
declaring—

> *I say as I have said long heretofore,*
> *I know but narrow freedom. Feel'st thou not*
> *We are in Its hands as he ?—Here, as elsewhere,*
> *We do but as we may ; no further dare.*[2]

The Spirit of the Pities must be continually reminded
that his intercessions in human affairs are futile.   Of
his desire to speak with Napoleon in order to abate
the misery of peoples, the Spirit of the Years says,
" Speak if thou wilt, whose speech nor mars nor
mends ! " [3]   When the repeated visualization of the
Will moves the Pities to expressions of the deepest
compassion the Ironic Spirits reply—

> *O Innocents, can ye forget*
> *That things to be were shaped and set*
> *Ere mortals and this planet met ?*
>
> *Stand ye apostrophizing* That*
> *Which, working all, works but thereat*
> *Like some sublime fermenting-vat . . . ?*[4]

And the Spirit of the Years offers them this questionable comfort—

> *Mild one, be not too touched with human fate.*
> *Such is the Drama ; such the Mortal State ;*
> *No sigh of thine can nul the Plan Predestinate !*[5]

[1] *Dynasts*, I, 1, i.   [2] I, 2, iii.   [3] II, 5, i.
[4] I, 6, iii.   [5] II, 6, v.

The whole universe of men, nations, and spirits, is conceived as an immense automatic clockwork, which, having been wound up once for all, must run its course according to the predetermined Plan. This simile, first expressed in the Fore-Scene, is many times repeated in the course of the drama.

An ironic effect of truly overwhelming intensity is produced, in view of the irresistible workings of the Autonomous Will, by the descriptions of men's elaborate plannings, and determinations, and purposes. The actors in the historical drama consider themselves free indeed ; yet they are only playthings in the hands of the Will. The speeches in the English Parliament, the political decisions of ministers and princes, the intricate web of mutual deception by lies, intrigues, treaties, and counter-treaties, spun out over the whole of Europe, individual and collective acts of heroism on the battlefield, and similar manifestations of a supposedly free will on the part of man, able to influence the course of events,—what are they but the movings of the tissues of one universal Brain ?

The tragic figure of Napoleon, in particular, is frequently endowed with the element of the ridiculous by his pompous recitals of his purposes, in view of the fact that the Intelligences and the readers recognize the powerlessness of any man to influence the foreordained issue. When Decres doubts whether Villeneuve's ships will arrive in time, the Emperor impatiently retorts—

> . . . But they will ; and do it early, too !
> There's nothing hinders them. My God, they must,
> For I have much before me when this stroke
> At England's dealt,[1]

[1] *Dynasts*, I, 2, iii.

and before Austerlitz his voice is heard, exhorting
the army—

> For victory, men, must be no thing surmised,
> As that which may or may not beam on us,
> Like noontide sunshine or a dubious morn ;
> It must be sure ! [1]

How violently he rails against destiny that his
" ripened plans," his " long-conned project " against
the British Isles, should come to nothing " as 'twere
a juvenile's snow-built device ! " But he is forced
to submit to a superior power and voice his resignation : " Well, have it so ! What are we going
to do ? " [2]

If the most heroic and tragic characters in *The
Dynasts* are examined, it will be discovered that the
wiser a man is, the higher his position, and the
heavier his apparent responsibility, the more clearly
he feels himself to be only a predestinate puppet and
a tool. The unfortunate Admiral Villeneuve has a
vague sense of an impending Destiny—

> *He pens in fits, with pallid restlessness,*
> *Like one who sees misfortune stalk the wave,*
> *And can nor face nor flee it.*[3]

Stronger fatalistic convictions and premonitions are
felt by Nelson. Before Trafalgar, he exclaims—

> And I have warnings, warnings, Collingwood,
> That my effective hours are shortening here ;
> Strange warnings now and then, as 'twere within me
> Which, though I fear them not, I recognize.[4]

Napoleon appears as an outspoken determinist. Although he can scoff at the Russians' conception of

[1] *Dynasts*, I, 6, 1.   [2] I, 3, i.   [3] I, 6, i.   [4] I, 2, i.

their " destiny," he opens his campaign against them
with these significant words—

> That which has worked will work !—Since Lodi Bridge
> The force I then felt moves me on
> Whether I will or no ; and oftentimes
> Against my better mind. . . . Why am I here ?
> —By laws imposed on me inexorably !
> History makes use of me to weave her web
> To her long while afore-time-figured mesh
> And contemplated charactery : no more.[1]

How deeply the reader of *The Dynasts* is struck by
the first phrase in these words : " That which has
worked will work ! " The Emperor, trying to
steady his courage and determination, gives utterance
to his belief that the same means which in the past
were sufficient for success will serve him in the future.
He does not know that as the mouthpiece of the
moving forces of the universe he has expressed a
deeper sense : that the Will which has worked out
all things in the past will continue to do so in the
future.

In his conversation with Queen Louisa of Prussia,
Napoleon's fatalistic convictions again come strongly
to the fore—

> Know you, my Fair,
> That I—ay, I—in this deserve your pity.—
> Some force within me, baffling mine intent,
> Harries me onward, whether I will or no.
> My star, my star is what's to blame—not I.
> It is unswervable !

—whereupon the Spirit of the Years delivers this
significant comment—

[1] *Dynasts*, III, i, ii.

" *Earth's Jackaclocks* "

He spoke thus at the Bridge of Lodi.   Strange,
He's of the few in Europe [1] *who discern*
The workings of the Will. [2]

Before Waterloo, when the apparition of the Duke
of Enghien presents to him a vision of the victims
of his ambitions, he cries—

> Why, why should this reproach be dealt me now?
> Why hold me my own master, if I be
> Ruled by the pitiless Planet of Destiny? [3]

It is not surprising, then, that Hardy in his fatalistic poem occasionally employs the old tragic trick
of quasi-supernatural premonitions of coming events.
Here again there is a remarkable parallelism between
him and Schopenhauer, who was a firm believer in
somnambulistic phenomena, visions, deuteroscopy,
and (to a certain extent) the significance of dreams. [4]
The Spirit of the Years sees clearly for some distance
into the future, and directly addresses the Duke of
Brunswick—

> *O Brunswick, Duke of Deathwounds!   Even as he*
> *For whom thou wearest that filial weedery*
> *Was waylaid by my tipstaff nine years since,*
> *So thou this day shalt feel his fendless tap,*
> *And join thy sire!*

> BRUNSWICK (starting up).

>   I am stirred by inner words,
> As 'twere my father's angel calling me,—
> That prelude to our death my lineage know! [5]

[1] It is just possible that Hardy realized, with Schopenhauer, the wide-
spread recognition of the Will among fatalistic Oriental thinkers, in thus
limiting to Europe a general ignorance of its workings and a prevalent
naïve acceptance of the notion of free will.

[2] *Dynasts,* II, 1, viii.   [3] III, 6, iv; cf. III, 7, viii.

[4] Schopenhauer, *Versuch ueber Geistersehen,* p. 319 sqq.

[5] *Dynasts,* III, 6, ii.

Not only Brunswick, but many other fated heroes are confronted with the fantastic spectre of Death before the Battle—[1]

SPIRIT OF PITIES.

When those stout men-at-arms drew doorward there,
I saw a like grimacing shadow march
And pirouette before no few of them.
Some of themselves beheld it ; some did not.

SPIRIT OF THE YEARS.

Which were so ushered ?

SPIRIT OF PITIES.

      Brunswick, who saw and knew ;
One also moved before Sir Thomas Picton,
Who coolly conned and drily spoke to it ;
Another danced in front of Ponsonby,
Who failed of heeding his.—De Lancey, Hay,
Gordon, and Cameron, and many more
Were footmanned by like phantoms from the ball.

SPIRIT OF THE YEARS.

Multiplied shimmerings of my Protean friend,
Who means to couch them shortly.[2]

The keenly intuitive feminine mind of the wife of Captain Prescott feels the foreordained tragedy that is to strike her. She exclaims, " The coming battle frightens me ! " and the Spirit of the Years notes that it is no ordinary fear that she experiences, but

This is her prescient pang of widowhood.
Ere Salamanca strike to-morrow's close
She'll find her consort stiff among the slain.[3]

---

[1] It is interesting to note the very similar spirit of the earliest heroic Anglo-Saxon poetry. Warriors are fated to live or to die before they enter the battle.
[2] *Dynasts*, III, 6, ii.
[3] III, 1, ii. In his frank employment of the device of " prophecy

Closely bound up with the deterministic implications of the doctrine of the Will is Hardy's attitude,
as a novelist, towards the problem of the possibility
of reformation or regeneration of character. Again
he is in perfect harmony with the views of Schopenhauer. No real change in character is at all possible
in a world in which man is, from his birth, controlled
by irresistible influences. *The Mayor of Casterbridge*,
Michael Henchard, is unable, for all his heroic and
high-minded efforts to overcome his destructive self-
will, which leads him finally to his grief and a
suicide's grave. The final "reformations" of Jude
the Obscure and of his soul's companion, Sue Bride-
head, the one returning to his lawful wife, the other
to her husband, are presented as ghastly travesties
on the supposed sanctity of the marriage-bond.
Reformation in the ordinary sense is here presented
as an actual defilement of body and soul.

Likewise the episode of Alec D'Urberville's "conversion" in *Tess* is merely a violent illustration of the
Schopenhauerian thesis that the action of a man may
change, but that his spiritual nature, his character,
remains what it always was. Thus the heroine
beholds her seducer turned reformer—

It was less a transformation than a transfiguration. The
former curves of sensuousness were now modulated to lines
of devotional passion. The lip-shapes that had meant seduc-
tiveness were now made to express divine supplication ; the
glow on the cheek that yesterday could be translated as
riotousness was evangelized to-day into the splendour of pious
enthusiasm ; animalism had become fanaticism ; Paganism

after the event " Hardy is in sympathy with the methods of Æschylus,
who makes his Prometheus, far back in the prehistoric past, foretell the
eruption of Ætna of the year 478 B.C. (*Prom.* 354 ff. See also Pindar,
Pyth. i, for a description of the same eruption). Note also that the Shade
of Darius sees the defeat of the Persian host before the arrival of the messenger
(*Pers.* 798–802).

Paulinism ; the bold, rolling eye that had flashed upon her shrinking form in the old time with such gross mastery now beamed with the rude energy of a righteousness that was almost ferocious. Those hard, black angularities which his face had used to put on when his wishes were thwarted by her modesty, now did duty in picturing the incorrigible back-slider who would insist upon turning again to his wallowing in the mire.

The lineaments, as such, seemed to complain. They had been divested from their hereditary connotation to signify impressions for which nature did not intend them. Strange that their very elevation was a misapplication, that to raise seemed to falsify.[1]

Another practical conclusion drawn from the doctrine of the Autonomous Will is a recognition of the futility of all remorse. The mental tortures of self-reproach form the ground-tone of such colourful and passionate poems as *The Torn Letter* (*SC*), *The Face at the Casement* (*SC*), and *The Woman in the Rye* (*SC*).[2] In *The Dynasts*, Nelson's profound dissatisfaction with himself is an impressive illustration of Schopenhauer's word, that discontent with one's self is the greatest of all pains.

Napoleon alone is so saturated with fatalism that he is incapable of feeling remorse. At Waterloo, despite the objections of the faithful Ney, he attempts to save the already hopeless situation by a lie ; he deceives the soldiery into thinking that Blucher's thirty thousand advancing Prussians are Grouchy's army, whereupon the Spirit Sinister remarks—

> *He tops all human greatness ; in that he*
> *To lesser grounds of greatness adds the prime*
> *Of being without a conscience.*[3]

[1] Chap. xlv.   [2] Quoted in chap. vi.   [3] *Dynasts*, III, 7, viii.

CHAPTER FIVE

"UNWEETING WHY OR WHENCE"

WITH THE GREATEST emphasis Schopenhauer voices his entire rejection of the position of earlier philosophers who had conceived of the essential nature of man as a thinking soul, and who recognized in it the reflection of some Superior Intelligence variously described as a personal Deity or an impersonal principle. Not a Supreme Intelligence but the all-energizing Will is the thing-in-itself underlying the phenomenal world, and this Will is unconscious. The unconsciousness of the Will follows by necessity from the fact that it is one. For consciousness or knowledge presupposes a difference between the knowing subject and the known object. Such difference, however, is only found in the world of perception, diversified in time and space. As thing-in-itself the Will is the all-in-all ; there is nothing beside it that it might comprehend in knowledge ; it is thus forever beyond consciousness as it is beyond time and space.[1]

Inorganic nature represents the lowest stage of the objectification of the Will, and here it appears as blind and unconscious striving, as an obscure and inarticulate impulse, manifesting itself in the operation of those original forces by which a multiplicity

[1] Sch. i, 169 ; ii, 324.

of phenomena without a trace of individual character is produced. From grade to grade objectifying itself more distinctly, yet still completely without consciousness as an obscure striving, the Will acts in the vegetable kingdom as well as in the vegetative part of the animal phenomenon, only that here, instead of the operation of irresistible causes as in inorganic nature, a definite reaction to stimuli can be observed. Finally the ascending grades of the objectification of the Will lead to a point at which the individual that expresses the idea can no longer receive food for its assimilation through movement following upon stimuli. " For such stimulus must be waited for ; but the food has now come to be of a more special and definite kind, and with the ever-increasing multiplicity of the individual phenomena the crowd and confusion have become so great that they interfere with each other, and the chances of the individual that is moved merely by stimuli and must wait for its food till such stimuli are presented, would be very small. From the point, therefore, at which the animal has delivered itself from the egg or the womb in which it vegetated without consciousness, its food must be sought out and selected. For this purpose movement following upon motive, and therefore consciousness, becomes necessary as an expedient for the preservation of the individual and the propagation of the species." [1]

Man in particular, this complicated highly organized, imaginative being of many needs, exposed to innumerable dangers, must, in order to exist, be provided with a double knowledge : Like the lower animals he must have perception by means of the senses, and in addition he must have reason as the faculty of framing abstract conceptions. With this

[1] Sch. i, 211.

there has appeared reflection, an ability to survey the future and the past, and as a consequence, deliberation, care, the power of premeditated action independent of the present, and the full and distinct consciousness of one's own deliberate volition as such.[1]

While conscious man thus represents the highest grade of the objectification of the Will, the possession of reason is, in another aspect, considered by Schopenhauer a distinct disadvantage. For will without consciousness followed its tendency with unerring certainty and infallible regularity in inorganic and merely vegetative nature. It acted alone according to its original nature, as a blind impulse, without assistance and without interruption from an entirely different world, the world of perception. With the entrance of reason, illusion, deception, irresolution, uncertainty, and error became possibilities, and in many cases obstructed the proper objectification of the Will in action. For although, in the human character, the Will has already taken its definite and unchangeable bent or direction, in accordance with which volition, when occasioned by the presence of a motive, invariably takes place, yet error can falsify its expressions, for it introduces illusive motives that take the place of the real ones which they resemble ; as, for example, when superstition forces on a man imaginary motives which impel him to a course of action directly opposed to the way in which the will would otherwise express itself in the given circumstances. Agamemnon slays his daughter ; a miser dispenses alms, out of pure egoism, in the hope that he will some day receive a hundredfold.[2]

[1] Sch. ii, 232 : *Vom Primat des Willens in Selbstbewusstsein.*
[2] Sch. i, 214.

However, important as is the function of the intellect, it cannot alter the fact that man according to Schopenhauer, is primarily a willing, and not a reasoning, being. As a strong blind man carries on his shoulders a lame man who can see, so blind will is the mighty force determining the course of human life, and makes use only to a certain extent of the light of reason as its medium of motives.[1] Originally the intellect is entirely a stranger to the purposes of the will. It supplies the motive to the will, but it only learns afterwards, completely *a posteriori*, how it has affected it, as one who makes a chemical experiment applies the reagents and awaits the result. Indeed, the intellect remains so completely excluded from the real decisions and secret purposes of its own will that sometimes it can only learn them like those of a stranger, by spying upon them and surprising them, and must catch the will in the act of expressing itself in order to get at its real intentions. Often we do not know what we wish or what we fear. A man may entertain a wish for years—for instance, for the death of a relative whose heir he expects to be—without ever confessing it to himself, or even allowing it to come to clear consciousness, for the intellect must know nothing about it, because the good opinion which he holds of himself might thereby suffer. But if the desired event happens he learns to his joy, not without shame, that he had wished it. Often we are in error as to the real motive from which we have done something or left it undone, till at last perhaps an accident discloses to us the secret and we know that what we have held to be the motive was not the true one, but another we had not wished to confess to ourselves,

[1] Sch. ii, 242.

because it by no means accorded with the good opinion we entertained of ourselves. Sometimes a man does not even guess at the true motive of his action, nay, does not believe himself capable of being influenced by such a motive, and yet it is the true motive of his action.[1]

The Will, then, is the original and metaphysical element in man, and the intellect is entirely subordinate to it. The Will is the wanderer carrying in his hands the intellect like a lantern. The wanderer does the walking, not the lantern. The Will is the constant element in man, constituting the identity of the person. Perceptions, opinions, convictions, and resolutions vary, but the Will as expressed through the character remains unchanged till the end.[2]

A significant application of these principles is found in Schopenhauer's theory of love. Divested of its romantic habiliments it is the instinctive urgency of the Will, emanating from the primary source of all being, intent upon the propagation of the race, striving to objectify itself in new individuals.[3]

One does not have to read very far in *The Dynasts* to gain the impression that Hardy is in full agreement with the doctrine of the Unconscious Will as outlined above, and that he, like Schopenhauer, has completely abandoned the conception of a Supreme Intelligence as the creative principle underlying the universe, an idea which had heretofore been one of the fundamentals of popular religion and of traditional philosophy, whether the principle was called God or the Absolute Mind. To Hardy's thought all things have originated in the inscrutable abyss of

[1] Sch. ii, 243 sqq.   [2] Sch. ii, 278.
[3] Sch. ii, 623 sqq., *Metaphysik der Geschlechtsliebe.*

Unconsciousness, and human intelligence is merely an incident in the chain of phenomena, coming into being through some caprice of circumstance.

"It works unconsciously, as heretofore," is the first definite statement made about the Immanent Will by the Spirit of the Years. It is "an automatic sense, unweeting why or whence." Hardy's answer to the age-old question of Isaiah, "Should he who made the eye not see, and he who made the mind not think?" is an outspoken "no." The Prime Energy underlying all phenomena of consciousness is but "a viewless, voiceless Turner of the Wheel," for ever weaving the intricate net of existence

> . . . *like a knitter drowsed*
> *Whose fingers play in skilled unmindfulness.*[1]

Thus the Will, unmaliced, unimpassioned, nescient,[2] loveless and hateless, a dreaming, dark, dumb Thing,[3] is entirely beyond all anthropomorphic attributes with which the sacred records of religion have ever invested the Supreme Being. Of the Eternal Wisdom of the theologians Hardy can detect no trace in the universe as he knows it. The lesson taught by history and by modern life is that of "life's impulsion by incognizance."[4] The Spirit of the Years with all his intellectual powers of discernment and prevision, representing as he does "the passionless insight of the ages," is but the "Eldest-Born of the Unconscious Cause,"[5] and when the Spirit Ironic observes that the Will, like a deft manipulator of lantern-slides, "might smile at his own art" in

---

[1] *Dynasts*, Fore-Scene. [2] II, 6, v. [3] After-Scene.
[4] I, 1, vi. "*Nothing appears of shape to indicate that Cognizance has marshalled things terrene*" (Fore-Scene).
[5] I, 2, iii.

bringing about Austria's collapse, the Chorus of the
Years answers—

> *Ah, no ; ah, no !*
> *It is impassible as glacial snow.—*
> *Within the Great Unshaken*
> *These painted shapes awaken*
> *A lesser thrill than doth the gentle lave*
> *Of yonder bank by Danube's wandering wave*
> *Within the Schwarzwald heights that give it flow !* [1]

Thought is indeed a phase of the Will's manifestations. The " Inadvertent Mind " [2] thinks on,
yet weighs not its thought.[3] It has purposes, just
as in Schopenhauer its purposiveness is traced in
the teleological arrangement of nature.[4] But it is
" tranced in its purpose to unknowingness," [5] and
its mental processes, if they may be called such, are
quite different from those of man. Even the Spirit
Ironic admits that

> *The groping tentativeness of an Immanent Will*
> *Cannot be asked to learn logic at this time of day.*[6]

When the Pities cannot help but question—

> *Why prompts the Will so senseless-shaped a doing ?*

the Spirit of the Years replies—

> *I have told thee that It works unwittingly,*
> *As one possessed, not judging,*

and the Chorus of Ironic Spirits give assent—

> *Of Its doings if It knew*
> *What It does It would not do !*

---

[1] *Dynasts*, I, 4, v.   [2] After-Scene.
[3] Yet Dr. Garwood sums up the whole Schopenhauer-Hardy scheme
under the term " purposelessness ! "
[4] *Dynasts*, I, 1, iii.   [5] II, 4, v.   [6] III, 7, viii.

Since It knows not, what far sense
Speeds Its spinnings in the Immense?
None; a fixed foresightless dream
Is Its whole philosopheme.
Just so, an unconscious planning,
Like a potter raptly panning! [1]

The Will, then, works with plans, purposes, and
"ceaseless artistries in Circumstance," but not as a
result of conscious reflection—

Thus doth the Great Foresightless mechanize
In blank entrancement now as evermore. [2]

The inexperienced Spirits of the Pities, reasoning
according to human standards of logic, are again and
again perplexed with the inevitable questionings that
arise out of this conception. Is the Great Cause
inferior to its creatures, and can anything exist in
the effects and by-products that was not originally
contained in the Cause? To this the Spirit of the
Years voices the poet's deepest conviction that there
exists within the Will, and ever has existed, something higher than human consciousness. The general
chorus of the Intelligences chants the supremacy of
the Will over the human intellect in the exact
Schopenhauerian sense, in the Fore-Scene—

The Prime that willed ere wareness was
Whose Brain perchance is Space, whose Thought its laws.

Having existed before intelligence, which it brought
forth through its inherent Energy, it must not be
conceived as a lower form of being, but as something
"scoped above percipience." [3] Even as Schopenhauer traces back the teleological arrangement of

[1] *Dynasts*, III, 7, viii.　　　[2] After-Scene.　　　[3] I, 1, vi.

116

nature to the " bewusstlose Allwissenheit der grossen Mutter," so does Hardy see in the universe a Power operating toward the realization of vast purposes, unmoved, however, by what mortals conceive as " motives "—

> . . *men's passions, virtues, visions, crimes,*
>   *Obey resistlessly*
> *The purposive, unmotived, dominant Thing*
> *Which sways in brooding dark their wayfaring !* [1]

The direction of its activity cannot be exactly defined as " purpose "—though it may be analogous to " purpose," it nevertheless exists on a higher plane. (It is elsewhere called, perhaps more correctly, " processive ": yet *purposive* may be held to mean no more.) The Intelligences discover its super-purposes, for instance, in Napoleon's suddenly darkening countenance during the celebration of his nuptials with Maria Louisa, ascribing this to the " sound artistry of the Immanent Will." [2] Ethically considered, it is beyond the sphere in which the moral conceptions of good and evil have any significance ; it is " past the sense of kindly eyed benevolence." [3] Its essential super-consciousness is perhaps most clearly expressed in the following words—

> *In that Immense unweeting Mind is shown*
> *One far above forethinking ; purposive,*
> *Yet superconscious ; a Clairvoyancy*
> *That knows not what it knows, yet works therewith* [4]

The presupposition that the Will was once conscious and later sank to a lower stage of existence is quickly dismissed at the opening of the poem. To

---

[1] *Dynasts,* II, 2, iii.   [2] II, 5, viii.
[3] After-Scene.   [4] I, 5, iv.

the question of the Pities, " Why doth It so and so, and ever so ? " the Spirit of the Years replies—

> *As one sad story runs, It lends Its heed*
> *To other worlds, being wearied out with this ;*
> *Wherefore Its mindlessness of earthly woes.*
> *Some, too, have told at whiles that rightfully*
> *Its warefulness, Its care, this planet lost*
> *When in her early growth and crudity*
> *By bad mad acts of severance men contrived,*
> *Working such nescience by their own device.—*
> *Yea, so it stands in certain chronicles,*
> *Though not in mine.*[1]

The Pities feel that the misery of man is chiefly due to the fact that he finds himself a conscious and suffering being in a universe ruled by an Unconscious Will. Therefore the questionable possibility of its becoming conscious is brought up again and again by them. If men gained cognition in the course of time, why not the Immense Power to which they owe their very being ?

> *Meet is it, none the less,*
> *To bear in thought that though Its consciousness*
> *May be estranged, engrossed afar, or sealed,*
> *Sublunar shocks may wake Its watch anon ?*

The only ray of hope discoverable for this unhappy world is thus expressed by the Pities—

> *Yet It may wake and understand*
> *Ere Earth unshape, know all things, and*
> *With knowledge use a painless hand,*
> *A painless hand !*[2]

That mundane events may vaguely influence the Prime Energy, and that human consciousness may

---

[1] *Dynasts*, Fore-Scene. Plainly a reference to the story of the Fall of Man, in *Gen.* iii. [2] II, 6, vii.

thus react in some mysterious way upon its Fundamental Cause, is the theme of the song of the Ironic
Spirits with which the birth of the Emperor's son
is celebrated—

> *The Will itself is slave to him,*
> *And holds it blissful to obey !—*
> *He said, " Go to ; it is my whim*
>
> *" To bed a bride without delay,*
> *Who shall unite my dull new name*
> *With one that shone in Cæsar's day.*
>
> *" She must conceive—you hear my claim ?—*
> *And bear a son—no daughter, mind—*
> *Who shall hand on my form and fame*
>
> *" To future times as I have designed ;*
> *And at the birth throughout the land*
> *Must cannon roar and alp-horns wind ! "*
>
> *The Will grew conscious at command,*
> *And ordered issue as he planned.*[1]

It must be observed that this indefinable idea is
expressed by the Ironic Spirits, and that its significance
is thus perhaps primarily satirical. The whole question : " Shall blankness be for aye ? " is felt by the
poet to press upon his heart and mind, but it is finally
left unanswered. He meditates upon the possibility
of the Will becoming conscious and thereby bringing
about a re-establishment of the harmony of the world,
while such a possibility is definitely excluded in the
system of Schopenhauer.

Although Hardy nowhere gives full expression to
the strictly Schopenhauerian theory of the origin of

---

[1] *Dynasts*, II, 6, iii (but this is, of course, merely ironic overstatement).

human consciousness, he will be seen, in his handling of men and motives, to be in full accord with the idea that intellect is not a basic endowment of the will but a single gear in the teleological machinery underlying the world-phenomena ; as the means by which the Will objectifies itself in man, consciousness pursues its ends by the light of reason in understanding and choosing between motives.

However, in man the intellect is completely subordinate, and the dominant will is absolutely supreme. The anthropomorphic Spirit of the Years knows that he is

> . . . *but an accessory of Its works*
> *Whom chance has rendered conscious ; and at most [I]*
> *Figure as bounden witness of Its laws.*[1]

and the Chorus of Intelligences confesses—

> *Our incorporeal sense*
> *Our overseeings, our supernal state,*
> *Our reasonings Why and Whence,*
> *Are but the flower of man's intelligence ;*
> *And that but an unreckoned incident*
> *Of the all-urging Will, raptly magnipotent.*[2]

One of the essentially tragic themes in the human action of the drama is humanity's unconsciousness of the larger movements in the great web of destiny, despite the modicum of intelligence that partially illumines the narrow channel of its wayfaring. This is felt particularly as the reader becomes aware of the satirical undertone that accompanies the presentation of the network of cunning diplomacy, the attempts of nations and their representatives to cheat friends and foes, veiling their purposes under vociferous

[1] *Dynasts*, I, 1, ii.   [2] I, 6, viii.

declarations of policy, secret treaties, and hypocritical assertions of non-responsibility for bloodshed.[1]

Every one of the human actors believes himself to be perfectly competent to survey and understand the situation fully, while the reader is made aware, with painful irony, that they are all blind leaders of the blind,—like sheep gone astray they are driven on by the Will in a cloud of self-deceptive consciousness. In the language of Schopenhauer, man as the objectification of the Autonomous Will, believes himself free while determined in everything, so does he believe himself, as the objectification of the Unconscious Will, to be fully conscious and aware of the course of events, while in reality only partially so.

The Will's unconsciousness is reflected in the uncertain and wavering decisions of the human actors. The fluctuating, instinctive, and unreasoning passions of the Berlin populace are thus interpreted—

> *Uncertainly, by fits, the Will doth work*
> *In Brunswick's blood, their chief, as in themselves.*[2]

The nation's distressed soul

> *. . . boils in a boisterous thrill*
> *Through the mart,*
> *Unconscious well-nigh as the Will*
> *Of its part :*
> *Would it wholly might be so, and feel not the forth-*
> *coming smart !*

> *In conclaves no voice of reflection*
> *Is heard*
> *King, councillors grudge circumspection*
> *A word,*
> *And victory is visioned, and seemings as facts are*
> *averred.*[3]

Dynasts, II, 1, iii.   [2] II, 1, iii.   [3] III, 6, iv.

No matter how self-important men and nations may deport themselves, they appear to the higher Intelligences merely as

> *Men—unnatured and mechanic-drawn—*
> *Mixt nationalities in row on row,*
> *Wheeling them to and fro*
> *In moves dissociate from their soul's demand. . . .*[1]

With all their vaunted power of reasoning they go about as in a dream—

> *Thus do the mindless minions of the spell*
> *In mechanized enchantment sway.*[2]

Even the greatest men are powerless to perceive the real significance of events or the vital issues that concern them. The Spirit of the Pities cannot understand that Napoleon should have no intimation of his future relationship with the Austrian court, to which he is irresistibly drawn by events—

> *Has he no heart-hints that this Austrian court,*
> *Whereon his mood takes mould so masterful,*
> *Is rearing naïvely in its nursery-room*
> *A future wife for him?*[3]

Everywhere it is apparent that, like Schopenhauer, Hardy conceives man not primarily as a thinking soul, but as a dimly striving will. A moment before Maria Louisa leaves Paris, thereby taking a step that leads unavoidably to her complete separation from Napoleon, she is represented as wavering, in great mental bewilderment, between going and staying. " I don't know what—what shall I do ? " she cries, and then makes the fateful decision not as a result of cool and clear reflection, but upon the impulse of unaccountable will.[4] Before Napoleon leaves Elba,

---

[1] *Dynasts*, II, 6, iv.   [2] III, 1, v.   [3] II, 5, ii.   [4] III, 4, iii.

we see his " halting hand and unlightened eye." [1]
The Spirit of the Pities voices the deepest thought
that underlies all human consciousness, as he asks,
" Where are we, and why are we where we are ? " [2]
To this fearful question no intelligence can supply
an adequate answer. The clearest exposition of the
idea that the will exercises supremacy over the intellect
in man is perhaps supplied by the representation of
Wellington in the last visualization of the Will at
Waterloo. The great commander is seen to be a
mere fibre in the Universal Brain like the meanest
and humblest of men, and to be " acting while dis-
covering his intention to act." Thus man does not
think first and then act, but he wills first, his will
determines upon action, and finally, as Schopenhauer
says, completely *a posteriori*, the intellect is informed
about the decisions of the will.[3]

Even more than *The Dynasts* do the novels of
Hardy illustrate the conception of man as a willing
rather than a thinking being and that he is ruled not
by reason but by the mysterious inclinations of his
nature. The will within him forces him on, often
against his better judgment. Thus do the passionate instincts of the Mayor of Casterbridge drive him
on to his ruin, thus does some inexplicable force draw
together Eustacia Vye and Damon Wildeve, and Tess
and Angel Clare, and thus is poor Jude torn away
unwillingly from his scholarly ambitions towards the
sensual Arabella as a recalcitrant schoolboy is dragged
along by the collar.

Particularly in his treatment of the theme of the
love of the sexes does Hardy follow the disillusioned

---

[1] *Dynasts*, III, 5, i.   [2] III, 1, viii.
[3] " Der Intellect erfährt die Beschluesse des Willens erst nachträ-
glich " (Sch. ii, 242).

Schopenhauerian view of the dominant Will. The laws of race-preservation, rather than ineffable spiritual forces control the situation. The extreme instance in *The Dynasts* is this ribald song with which the Ironic Spirits comment on Napoleon's marriage with the Austrian princess—

> *First 'twas a finished coquette,*
> *And now it's a raw ingénue.—*
> *Blonde instead of brunette,*
> *An old wife doffed for a new ;*
> > *She'll bring him a baby*
> > *As quickly as maybe,*
> *And that's what he wants her to do,*
> > > *Hoo-hoo !*
> *And that's what he wants her to do !*

SPIRIT OF THE YEARS.

What lewdness lip those wry-formed phantoms there ?

IRONIC SPIRITS.

Nay, Showman Years, With holy reverent air
We hymn the nuptials of the Imperial pair.[1]

In the lyric poems, perhaps, one might expect a somewhat different treatment of the eternal poets' theme of romantic love. In reading through *More Love-Lyrics* (TL) we find indeed a romantic atmosphere, and an artificiality that reminds us at times of the Elizabethan lyrists, but when the ardent poet ceases to feel spontaneously and begins to think, we find him lapsing into a mood of disillusion and renunciation that recalls Schopenhauer's unidealistic viewpoint, and that is best studied in the poem *I Said to Love* (PP).

[1] *Dynasts*, II, 5, vi.

It follows naturally, then, that we find the institution of marriage looked upon as a snare and a tyranny—as the fell destroyer of love and its delights. In *The Burghers* (*WP*) the enlightened husband gives his wife and her lover their freedom, considering himself but the " licensed tyrant of the bonded pair " ; in *A Wife and Another* (*TL*) the legal wife, similarly enlightened, sees herself as the snarer and her husband and his mistress as the trapped ; in *Over the Coffin* (*SC*) the two women voice the wish that " scorning parochial ways," they had " lived like the wives in the patriarchs' days." Splendid companion-studies to the scathing criticism of the institution found in Jude the Obscure are afforded by such poems as *The Curate's Kindness* (*TL*), *The Conformers* (*TL*), and *Long Plighted* (*PP*), while the temporary quality of the passion that often causes a permanent, and hence unfortunate, alliance, is made the basis of this triolet—

> If hours be years the twain are blest,
> For now they solace swift desire
> By bonds of every bond the best
> If hours be years. The twain are blest,
>
> Do eastern stars slope never west
> Nor pallid ashes follow fire :
> If hours be years the twain are blest,
> For now they solace swift desire.[1]

Hardy's conception of woman and her place in the universe is, even in the novels and stories, so foreign to the accepted idealization of other imagi-

---

[1] *At a Hasty Wedding* (*PP*). Used in the short story, *A Changed Man*, 1900.

native writers that many a fair dame has sworn eternal enmity to him. In such a powerful poem as *A Trampwoman's Tragedy* (*TL*), the reader will also find the mainspring of the disastrous course of events to be the woman's uncontrollable impulse to wanton and fickle acts of perverse wickedness. She seems to be displayed as an example of the arbitrary perversity of the Will in the human personality. Her irresistible evil instincts are not to be held against her, because she is made to suffer from them in the end quite as much as her victims. The pathos of the retributive consequences of her mutability is expressed in a very fine dramatic dialogue, *The Memorial Brass : 186–* (*MV*). Her concealment of a " past," a motif so often effectively used in the novels, is the foundation for such differing pieces as *The Husband's View* (*TL*) and *Rose-Ann* (*TL*). *The Sweet Hussy* (*SC*) is a defence of the male sex against the prevalent notion that the man is always the deceiver and the woman the beguiled,[1] and the poet's " dangerous insight into the female heart " can be well studied in *The Rival* (*MV*). When Hardy writes a poem on the vanity and heartlessness of woman he can compress into twelve short lines as much thought and feeling as are expended in the whole exposition of, say, Arabella in *Jude the Obscure*, witness *The Pink Frock* (*MV*)—

> " O my pretty pink frock,
>   I shan't be able to wear it !
>   Why is he dying just now ?
>   I hardly can bear it !

---

[1] Cf. *On the Tree of Knowledge*, May 1894, in *The New Review*, where Hardy writes : " . . . Innocent youths should, I think, also receive the same instruction ; for (if I may say a word out of my part) it has never struck me that the spider is invariably male and the fly invariably female."

"*Unweeting Why or Whence*"

"He might have contrived to live on ;
   But they say there's no hope whatever :
   And must I shut myself up,
      And go out never ?

"O my pretty pink frock !
   Puff-sleeved and accordion-pleated !
   He might have passed in July,
      And not so cheated ! "

CHAPTER SIX

THE ULTIMATE HOPE

EVERY SEPARATE ACT of the Will responds to a certain motive and aims at a certain object. What, then, is the final purpose towards which the Will as a whole is reaching forth, and what is the ultimate goal to be attained by this universal striving lying at the base of all phenomena ? Schopenhauer answers that the Will is aimless. Every man has permanent aims and motives by which his conduct is guided, and he is always in a position to give an account of his particular actions ; but if he were asked, why he wills at all, or why in general he wills to exist, he would have to confess that he does not know, and the question itself would appear to him meaningless. Indeed freedom from all aims and absence of all limits belongs to the nature of the Will whose very essence is an endless striving. The aimlessness of the Will discloses itself in its simplest form in the lowest grade of its objectification, in gravitation, which we see constantly exerting itself, though a final goal is obviously unattainable to it. This is precisely the case with all tendencies of all phenomena of the Will : every attained end is also the beginning of a new course, and so on *ad infinitum*. The Will manifesting itself in the plant, for instance, proceeds from the seed through the stem and the leaf to the blossom and the fruit, which again is the beginning of a new seed, and so on through endless time. Eternal becoming, endless flux, characterizes the revelation of the inner nature of the Will. When the Will is enlightened by knowledge, as in man, it always knows what it wills under certain conditions, but never, what it wills in general. Every particular act of Will has its end ; the Will as a whole is totally aimless.[1]

The recognition of the aimlessness of the Will forms the basis of Schopenhauer's pessimism, the deep conviction that all life is essentially suffering.[2] The real existence of man is only in the present, whose unchecked flight into the past is a constant transition into death, a constant dying. For his past life, apart from its possible consequences for the present, and the testimony regarding the character that is expressed in it, is now entirely done with, dead, and no longer anything real, whether its content was pain or pleasure. But the present is always passing through his hands into the past ; the future is quite uncertain and always short. Thus the existence of man, even considered from its formal side, is a constant hurrying of the present into the dead past—" ein stetes Hinstuerzen der Gegenwart in die tote Vergangenheit,"—a constant dying.[3] If we look at life from the physical side, it is clear that, as walking is merely a constantly prevented falling, life is only a constantly prevented dying, an ever-postponed death, as the activity of mind is a constantly deferred " Langeweile." Every breath we draw wards off the death that is constantly intruding upon us. We fight death with every meal we eat, with every hour of sleep we manage to take. Yet in the end it will

---

[1] Sch. i, 228 sqq.   [2] Sch. i, 403 sqq.   [3] Sch. i, 403.

conquer us, for we became subject to it through birth, and it only plays with its prey for a short while before finally swallowing it. However, we pursue our life with great interest and much solicitude as long as possible, as we blow a soap-bubble as long and as large as we can, although we are all the time aware that in the end it will burst.

Willing and striving is an unquenchable thirst, and the basis of all willing is need, deficiency, and pain. Thus all life is, originally and through its very being, subject to pain. If, on the other hand, it lacks objects of desire, because it is deprived of them by a too easily attained satisfaction, it becomes the victim of a terrible void and *ennui*, and life itself becomes an unbearable burden. Thus life swings like a pendulum back and forth between pain and satiety. Pain and satiety are indeed the ultimate ingredients of life. Pain is positive, but pleasure and happiness are negative in character—mere absence of pain,—and while popular belief relegated all pains and tortures to hell, it had nothing left for heaven but " Langeweile." [1]

It is really incredible how meaningless, dull, and obtuse is the life of the great majority of men. It is a weary longing and travailing, a dream-like staggering through the four ages to death. Ordinary men are like a clockwork, which is wound up and goes, it knows not why ; and every time a man is born, the clock of life is wound up anew, to repeat the same old piece it has played innumerable times before, passage after passage, measure after measure, with insignificant variations. The ordinary individual is but another short dream of the endless spirit of nature, of the persistent Will to live ; is only another

[1] Sch. i, 404, 414 sq.

fleeting form, which it carelessly sketches on its infinite page : time and space. However, the fate of the intellectually more highly developed man, Schopenhauer thinks, is more deplorable still. In proportion as knowledge ascends and consciousness attains to distinctness, susceptibility to pain also increases, and those who are gifted with genius suffer most of all, according to the saying of the Preacher : *Qui auget scientiam auget dolorem.*[1]

The life of every individual, if surveyed as a whole, and regarded in its significant features, is really always a tragedy, but considered in the details, it presents a ludicrous aspect. For the vexations of the day, the restless irritation of the moment, the desires and fears of every week, the mishaps and calamities of every hour, the pranks and tricks of chance bear the character of a hideous comedy. But the unsatisfied wishes, the frustrated efforts, the hopes unmercifully crushed by fate, the unfortunate errors of the whole life, with the ever higher rising tide of suffering and despair, and grim death waiting at the end, are the elements of the most fearful tragedy. Thus, as if fate had intended to add derision to the misery of existence, our life must contain all the elements of tragedy, yet we cannot even maintain the dignity of tragic characters, but in the broad detail of life, must inevitably appear as foolish characters of a comedy.[2]

Life, then, is a business that does not cover its costs. Like all bad merchandise, it is sometimes covered over with a false lustre, yet its utter emptiness and vanity cannot long remain hidden. Everyone who has awakened from the first dream of youth and who has considered his own experience and that

[1] Sch. i, 402. [2] Sch. i, 417.

of others will, if his judgment is not paralysed by some indelibly imprinted prejudice, arrive at the conclusion that this world is the kingdom of chance and error, which rule without mercy in things great and small, and alongside of which folly and wickedness wield the scourge. Every biography is a recital of suffering, for every life is, as a rule, a series of great and small misfortunes, which the sufferer conceals as much as possible, because he knows that others seldom can feel sympathy and compassion, but almost always satisfaction at the sight of the woes from which they themselves for the moment are exempt. At the end of life, if a man is sincere and in full possession of his faculties, he will never wish to live it over again, but rather than this he will much prefer absolute annihilation. Herodotus spoke the truth when he said that no man ever lived who did not wish more than once that he might not have to live the following day. The brevity of life, which is so constantly lamented, is after all the best quality it possesses.[1]

The pessimism of Schopenhauer which undoubtedly had its roots in the peculiar temperament of the philosopher and was occasioned by his environment and the conditions of the times, will appear to the average thinker as a one-sided view of life in the presentation of which the imagination of the author perhaps played as large a rôle as his reasoning mind. There is ample evidence, too, that Schopenhauer himself did not find the mental tranquillity born of absolute conviction in the dismal picture as the final goal of his thoughts. Throughout his writings the careful reader may detect an uncertain groping, a half-concealed striving for a higher goal, faint glimpses

[1] Sch. i, 419-22.

of a purer light appearing now and then on the horizon
of his gloomy speculations, that seem to hold out to
mankind the promise of a better hope.

It is in the nature of a welcome relief that the
reader, in spite of the assertions that this world is
thoroughly bad, in fact so bad that it could not exist
at all, were it just a little bit worse, frequently en-
counters expressions in which Schopenhauer gives
voice to his admiration for the teleological arrangement in nature and declares, that it is " wonderful in
its perfection." Although he declares that constant
misery is the lot of man, he speaks of the " pure
happiness of knowledge,"—" das reine Glueck des
willensfreien Erkennens,"—and the whole third section of his chief work gives convincing evidence that
he with innumerable others has experienced it.[1]
The antagonistic attitude of superficial, dim-eyed
critics could not destroy his firm faith in the ultimate
victory of truth. " The power of truth," he says,
" is incredibly great and of unspeakable endurance.
We find constant traces of it in all, even the most
eccentric and absurd dogmas of different times and
different lands,—often indeed in strange company,
curiously mixed up with other things, but still recog-
nizable. It is like a plant that germinates under a
heap of great stones, but still struggles up to the
light, working itself through with many deviations
and windings, disfigured, worn-out, stunted in its
growth,—but yet, to the light." [2] And the reader
feels that the world in which such a thing happens
cannot be the worst of all possible worlds. With
enthusiastic eloquence he extols pity and compassion
as the basis of true morality,—" boundless pity for
all living things, animals, strangers, personal enemies,

[1] Sch. i, 415.   [2] Sch. i, 196.

the ignorant, the depraved, even those who do not deserve it,"—and he professes to know no better prayer than the one which is found at the end of many ancient Hindu plays : "May all living things be delivered from their pain." And again we feel that life, after all, must be worth living if only for the reason that it enables us to contribute our humble share to this universal ministry of pity.[1]

The clearest indication of an ultimate hope, however, is found in those sections of Schopenhauer's writings where he develops his significant theory of the indestructibility of the Will. Will is the thing-in-itself, the inner content, and the real essence of the world as of every human being. Life, the visible world, is only the mirror of the Will. Therefore life accompanies the Will as inseparably as the shadow accompanies the body ; and if there is an eternal Will, there is also eternal life. As long as man is filled with the will to live, he need have no fear for his existence, even in the presence of death. As in all mental phenomena the form vanishes while the matter remains, so the individual consciousness of man becomes extinct, but the Will that actuated him will live on. To think that the real essence of man were annihilated in death would be as foolish as to infer the death of the spinner from the stopping of the spinning-wheel.[2] For the ceasing of the individual consciousness is by no means identical with the destruction of the principle of life manifesting itself in it. Every individual is transitory only as a phenomenon, but as thing-in-itself is timeless, and therefore endless. As phenomenon only the individual is distinguished from the other things of the world ; as

[1] Sch iii, 586 sqq. *Das Fundament der Moral.*
[2] Sch. i, 371.

thing-in-itself it is Will, the Will which appears in all, and death only destroys the illusion by which his consciousness separates itself from the rest. Man therefore need have no fear of death. Epicurus spoke the truth when he said : " Ὁ θάνατος μηδὲν πρὸς ἡμᾶς. For while we are, death is not ; and when death is, we are not." " Der Mensch hat den Tod so wenig zu fuerchten als die Sonne die Nacht." [1]

It is true that these ideas are far removed from the hope of immortality that religion holds out to man, but they give ample testimony to the significant fact that Schopenhauer no less than other thinking men keenly felt the *horror vacui* and instinctively shrank back from the final implications of a system that seemed to lead into the starless night of the " Nothing."

The fact that man, a being endowed with an unlimited capacity for consciousness and suffering, is made to live out his life in a universe ruled by an unconscious and indifferent Will, lies at the base of all of Hardy's so-called pessimism, and results in the essential tragedy of human existence. The Spirit of the Years bewails the " intolerable antilogy of making figments feel," and even the Spirit Ironic assents : " Logic's in that. It does not, I must own, quite play the game." [2] Thus do mortals innocently suffer an unjust fate imposed by an unreasoning Will—

> *But out of tune the Mode and meritless*
> *That quickens sense in shapes whom, thou hast said,*
> *Necessitation sways ! A life there was*
> *Among the self-same frail ones—Sophocles—*
> *Who visioned it too clearly, even the while*
> *He dubbed the Will the " gods." Truly said he,*

[1] Sch. i, 371.   [2] *Dynasts*, I, 4, vi.

" Such gross injustice to their own creation
Burdens the time with mournfulness for us,
And for themselves with shame."—Things mechanized
By coils and pivots set to foreframed codes
Would, in a thorough-sphered melodic rule,
And governance of sweet consistency,
Be cessed no pain, whose burnings would abide
With That which holds responsibility,
Or inexist.[1]

It is a similar train of thought that evokes from
Hardy expressions of passionate pity for the unfortunate and innocent Durbeyfield children, involuntary
passengers on a dismal voyage.[2]

The aimless strivings of the Unconscious Will are
to some extent manifested in the purposeless strivings
and sufferings in the life of man. The Will is perhaps not without aims, but they are " listless aims." [3]
It is forever turning the endless Wheel of Existence,
weaving its eternal artistries in Circumstance ; so
the Shade of the Earth can discover in the convulsions
of history but a painful travailing in " vain and
objectless monotony."[4] The Spirit Sinister is sure
that Father Years with all his wisdom could not till
Doomsday discover rhyme or reason in the world,[5]
and when indeed the sage contemplates the vastness
of the universe in which monsters of magnitude hang
" amid deep wells of nothingness " and human life
is but of scantest size, he finds that as far as reason
can tell, all this is " inutile." [6]

It is hardly necessary to demonstrate Hardy's
painful insistence on the useless sufferings and
miseries that accompany his pictures of humanity.
The reader of the novels, lyrics, and *Dynasts* cannot

[1] *Dynasts,* I, 5, iv. [2] *Tess,* chap. iii. [3] *Dynasts,* Fore-Scene.
[4] I, 1, ii. [5] I, 1, vi. [6] After-Scene.

escape the fearful questioning of the Shade of the Earth at Walcheren—

> *What storm is this of souls dissolved in sighs*
> *And what the dingy doom it signifies ?* [1]

So convincing is the tragic panorama, with its lesson driven home alike by *a priori* reasoning and by a concretely realized and unfortunately true and faithful view of humanity, that Hardy's pessimism is the prevailing impression that remains with his readers. This " mock-life," [2] through which the pitiful human clowns and misfits are relentlessly dragged, might, as the Spirit of the Pities declares when contemplating the sufferings of the old English King—

> *. . . drive Compassion past her patiency*
> *To hold that some mean, monstrous ironist*
> *Had built this mistimed fabric of the Spheres*
> *To watch the throbbings of its captive lives,*
> *(The which may Truth forfend), and not thy said*
> *Unmaliced, unimpassioned, nescient Will !* [3]

The soldier who is driven mad by the gruesome experiences during the retreat from Moscow has sense enough to realize that this is a foolish life and to bid it a cheerful adieu, while his companions are unhappier in their sanity ; tears are observed to remain in strings of ice upon their dead cheeks as they are discovered the following morning.[4] The chorus which chants the close of the bloody battle of Albuera thus epitomizes the tragic aspect of life—

> *They strove to live, they stretch to die,*
> *Friends, foemen, mingle ; heap and heap.—*
> *Hide their hacked bones, Earth !—deep, deep, deep,*

[1] *Dynasts*, II, 4, viii.   [2] III, 1, x.   [3] II, 6, v.   [4] III, 1, xi.

Where harmless worms caress and creep.—
What man can grieve? what woman weep?
Better than waking is to sleep! Albuera! [1]

Annihilation and non-existence are indeed felt to
be preferable to the inevitable miseries of life. The
Shade of the Earth looks at the futile struggle of
history and questions the value of all its " vain and
objectless monotony "—

When all such tedious conjuring could be shunned
By uncreation? Howsoever wise
The governance of these massed mortalities,
A juster wisdom his who should have ruled
They had not been.[2]

And the Spirit of the Pities exclaims—

Would I had not broke nescience, to inspect
A world so ill-contrived! [3]

The undeserved doom in the fiat " Thou shalt be
born," which is visited upon all the children who
come into the world was already given fine expression
in a poem written to secure aid for the poor of the
city, who are

Launched into thoroughfares too thronged before,
Mothered by those whose protest is " No more ! "
Vitalized without option : who shall say
That did Life hang on choosing—Yea or Nay—
They had not scorned it with such penalty,
And nothingness implored of Destiny ? [4]

---

[1] *Dynasts*, II, 6, iv.   [2] I, 1, ii.
[3] It is possible also to discern an echo of Schopenhauer's opinion that
this world could not exist at all if it were only slightly worse than it really
is, in the words of the Spirit Sinister's warning to the Spirit Ironic not to
carry his ironies too far—

Or you may wake up the Unconscious Itself, and tempt
It to let all the clockwork of the show run down in spite of us.

[4] *Lines (WP)*, 1890.

The Ultimate Hope

A little-known letter [1] written by Hardy to the Academy on M. *Maeterlinck's Apology for Nature* stresses the essential immorality of the quandary in which man finds himself in the world as it is constituted.

Sir,—

In your review of M. Maeterlinck's book you quote with seeming approval his vindication of Nature's ways, which is (as I understand it) to the effect that, though she does not appear to be just from our point of view, she may practise a scheme of morality unknown to us, in which she is just. Now, admit but the bare possibility of such a hidden morality, and she would go out of court without the slightest stain on her character, so certain should we feel that indifference to morality was beneath her greatness.

Far be it from my wish to distrust any comforting fantasy, if it be barely tenable. But alas, no profound reflection can be needed to detect the sophistry in M. Maeterlinck's argument, and to see that the original difficulty recognized by thinkers like Schopenhauer, Hartmann, Haeckel, etc., and by most of the persons called pessimists remains unsurmounted.

Pain has been, and pain is ; no new sort of morals in Nature can remove pain from the past and make it pleasure for those who are its infallible estimators, the bearers thereof. And no injustice, however slight, can be atoned for by her future generosity, however ample, so long as we consider Nature to be, or to stand for, unlimited power. The exoneration of an omnipotent Mother by her retrospective justice becomes an absurdity when we ask, what made the foregone injustice necessary to her Omnipotence ?

So you cannot, I fear, save her good name except by assuming one of two things : that she is blind and not a judge of her actions, or that she is an automaton, and unable to

---

[1] In *The Academy and Literature,* London, May 17, 1902. It has reference to a review of Maeterlinck's *The Buried Temple* (translated by Alfred Sutro), in particular his essay on " The Mystery of Justice which appeared in *The Academy* on May 3, 1902.

control them ; in either of which assumptions, though you have the chivalrous satisfaction of screening one of her sex, you only throw responsibility a stage further back.

But the story is not new. It is true, nevertheless, that, as M. Maeterlinck contends, to dwell too long amid such reflections does no good, and that to model our conduct on Nature's apparent conduct, as Nietzsche would have taught, can only bring disaster to humanity.

Yours truly,

Thomas Hardy.

Max Gate, Dorchester.

Perhaps the most poignant and terrible expression of the aimless and monotonous tragedy of existence may be found in the words by which the final visualization of the Will is portrayed in *The Dynasts*. After the curtain has finally gone down on the stupendous drama of battles, intrigues, sufferings, tears, and rivers of blood, the reader feels that for all its painful sound and harassing fury it signifies— nothing. Just as in the Fore-Scene to the tragic display, Europe is again observed as " a prone and emaciated figure," unchanged by any of the stormy woes that have tortured the poor humanity that continues ever to bleed and suffer to no avail.

In so far as comedy may be viewed as a ghastly punctuation and emphasis by contrast of the dominant undertone of existence, life is viewed by Hardy as well as by Schopenhauer as an inseparable welter of tragedy and comedy. " Let this terrestrial tragedy——," begins the Spirit of the Pities, whereupon the Spirit Ironic interrupts, " Nay, comedy."[1] " There's comedy in all things," remarks one of Napoleon's servants apropos of Josephine's misfortunes, and English officers, before the slaughter of Waterloo, dance to

[1] *Dynasts*, Fore-Scene.

the tune, " The Prime of Life." [1]   In the novels, the
application of the principle of comic relief in the
Wessex-peasantry-episodes is a further illustration of
the artistic value of bringing home the heartbreaking
tragedy all the more forcibly by setting it off against
a contrasting background.

It seems somewhat curious that Hardy has occasionally indicated that he does not particularly enjoy
being called a " pessimist." He thinks that his view
of life is the only possible one, but he is slow to admit
that he looks at life through darkened lenses.   It has
frequently been noted that he indicates at times that
there may exist loopholes of escape from the prison
of despair ; that there may be after all an ultimate
hope for a world in misery and travail.   This rather
vaguely defined hope or faith in the ultimate right-
ness of things takes three general forms : the Nirwana
of non-existence, the growth of consciousness in the
Will, and a melioristic belief in a gradual improvement in life through the idealistic efforts of enlightened
men.

Hardy definitely subscribes to the rather forlorn
hope that finds its foundation in a Schopenhauerian
renunciation of the Will to live.   He looks forward
with complacency, if not delight, to a future of endless unconsciousness whereby the harmony between
human life and the unconsciously governed universe
will be re-established.   The unhappy Villeneuve
hopes by his suicide to enter a blissful state of imper-
cipience, and the Spirit of the Pities thus pronounces
the last words over his body—

May his sad sunken soul merge into nought
Meekly and gently as a breeze at eve.[2]

The former Austrian Empress, enjoying Nirwana, is undisturbed by the tumult of the coronation—

> *Senseless of hustlings in her former house,*
> *Lost to all count of crowns and bridalry—*
> *Even of her Austrian blood.*[1]

" How know the coffined what comes after them ? " cries the Spirit Ironic to the Pities' imagined hearing of the voices of the dead,[2] and although Death in a thousand motley forms may still exhibit the passions of love and hatred, the souls of the slain have passed " to where history pens no page." [3] " Better than waking is to sleep," say the Pities.[4]

This idea of the anticipation of the joy in annihilation of personality had already received wonderful and perfect expression in *Friends Beyond* (*WP*), where it is applied to the happy dead of a peaceful country community. Neither squire nor fiddler feels any more the disturbing urge of life, with its desires, dreams, and passions.

Hardy is nevertheless occasionally attracted by the prevalent notions of survival, although he nowhere subscribes to them. The only immortality that exists for him is the ever-fading memory that lives after in the minds of friends and loved ones of the dead. This is to be found in many a poem, beginning with *Her Immortality* (*WP*), in which the poet cries to the vision of his beloved—

> " . . . My days are lonely here ;
>   I need thy smile alway :
> I'll use this night my ball or blade,
>   And join thee ere the day."

---

[1] *Dynasts*, II, 5, viii.   [2] III, 7, viii.
[3] III, 1, xi.   [4] II, 6, v.

The Ultimate Hope

A tremor stirred her tender lips,
  Which parted to dissuade :
" That cannot be, O friend," she cried ;
  " Think, I am but a Shade !

" A Shade but in its mindful ones
  Has immortality ;
By living, me you keep alive,
  By dying you slay me.

" In you resides my single power
  Of sweet continuance here ;
On your fidelity I count
  Through many a coming year."

—I started through me at her plight,
  So suddenly confessed :
Dismissing late distaste for life,
  I craved its bleak unrest.

" I will not die, my One of all !—
  To lengthen out thy days
I'll guard me from minutest harms
  That may invest my ways ! "

She smiled and went. Since then she comes
  Oft when her birth-moon climbs,
Or at the season's ingresses,
  Or anniversary times ;

But grows my grief. When I surcease,
  Through whom alone lives she,
Her spirit ends its living lease,
  Never again to be ! [1]

Nevertheless he indulges in a considerable amount
of toying with the idea of actual survival, which he

[1] See also the companion poem to this one, *His Immortality* (*PP*), and
The To-Be-Forgotten (*PP*).

143

almost seems prone to accept in *Transformations*
(*MV*) ; and in *The Masked Face* (*MV*) he stresses
the insolubility of the whole baffling enigma of life
and death. He seems throughout to be unsatisfied
with the results of strict scientific reasoning, and to
long for a more clairvoyant insight into the ideal
world—for

> The visioning powers of souls who dare
> To pierce the material screen [1]

A second, and entirely independent line of thought
which seems to indicate something akin to faith, is
that of the possibility of the harmony of the universe
being re-established through a growth of consciousness in the Immanent Will. This—quite anti-
Schopenhauerian—idea is not expressed as a conviction, but is only tentatively advanced as the forlorn
hope of the irrational Pities. The possibility of the
wakening of a kindly consciousness in the Will
through the reaction upon it of its conscious earthling-
figments, and the ensuing rule of painlessness, is
rather vaguely touched upon in various places.[2] If
men gained cognition with the flux of time, then why
not the Will to which they owe their very being ?—
thus do the Pities argue ; [3] they pray to some great
understanding Heart, in spite of the ridicule of the
other Intelligences,[4] and almost charm the passionless
Spirit of the Years " out of his strong-built thought "
with their ecstatic pæan of hope, one of the high-
water marks of all of Hardy's poetry. One almost
feels that Hardy himself joins in the final general
chorus of the Intelligences with which the work with

---

[1] *The House of Silence* (*MV*).   [2] E.g. I, 1, iii.
[3] *Dynasts*, After-Scene.   [4] II, 6, v.

all its gloom is brought to a conclusion in a brilliant major-chord—

> *But—a stirring thrills the air*
> *Like the sounds of joyance there*
> > *That the rages*
> > *Of the ages*
> *Shall be cancelled, and deliverance offered from the darts*
> > *that were,*
> *Consciousness the Will informing, till It fashion all things*
> > *fair!*

The third and final line of thought that seems to point toward an ultimate hope is still less in keeping with the general tenor of the rest of the Hardy philosophy. This is the prospect of the gradual improvement to be brought about by the conscious and directed efforts of men. According to the Pities—

> *The pale pathetic peoples still plod on*
> *Through hoodwinkings to light.*[1]

If, for the moment, we look outside his imaginative work and accept as authentic Mr. William Archer's *Real Conversation* with Hardy, we shall find a rather remarkable statement of a practical philosophy of living, that is in many ways distinctly antipathetic to the inevitable conclusions derived from the *Dynasts*-philosophy.[2]

" The world often seems to me," said Hardy to Mr. Archer, "like a half-expressed, an ill-expressed idea. . . . There may be a consciousness, infinitely afar off, at the other end of phenomena, always striving to express itself, and always baffled and blundering, just as the spirits seem to be. . . .

---

[1] *Dynasts* III, 4, iv.
[2] William Archer, *Real Conversations.* But Mr. Hardy does not admit that he spoke exactly as Mr. Archer here represents him as speaking.

My pessimism, if pessimism it be, does not involve the assumption that the world is going to the dogs, and that Ahriman is winning all along the line. On the contrary, my practical philosophy is distinctly meliorist. What are my books but one plea against 'man's inhumanity to man,' to woman—and to the lower animals. . . . Whatever may be the inherent good or evil of life, it is certain that men can make it much worse than it need be. When we have got rid of a thousand remediable ills, it will be time enough to determine whether the ill that is irremediable outweighs the good."

This seems to suggest a disregard for the fundamental philosophy expressed in his imaginative work. It is indeed hardly in human nature to accept the Will-theory completely and in all its manifestations and practical implications. Inconsistencies are inevitably discovered in the lives and works of professed determinists and pessimists. In Hardy's discussion with Mr. Archer of what is popularly known as the supernatural, for instance, he assured his interlocutor that he would give ten years of his life for the privilege of beholding an authentic and indubitable ghost.[1] Now if he really believed that " it is better never to have been born " (as he told Mr. Archer), how could he possibly consider ten years of his life in this alternately idiotic and malignant world as a commodity of any value whatsoever ? Why not rather ten years of extinction ?

That he is an ardent meliorist there can be no doubt, and there is a vast gulf between meliorism and pessimism. He certainly believes in the salutary lessons that history can teach—otherwise *The Dynasts* would have no reason for existence. This becomes even more manifest when we read the Prologue and the Epilogue written for the 1914 production, in

[1] Op. cit., p. 37.

which an attempt is made to use the teachings of the work as an inspiration and a guide to conduct in a present crisis. Likewise in the most pessimistic novels, *Tess* and *Jude*, there is implied the hope that the world will become happier when the laws of man are made to conform more closely to the laws, or impulses, of nature.

Again and again the elaborate system of pessimism breaks down, for Hardy seems to feel the *horror vacui* quite as distinctly as Schopenhauer. The indestructibility of the Will is reflected in the frequency with which Hardy applies to it the epithet " Eternal," and in the image of the Wheel, which signifies infinity.

Of the sour and cynical sort of pessimism there is remarkably little to be found in Hardy, despite all that commentators say. He does indeed believe in telling at all times the unadulterated truth, which is, according to Oscar Wilde, rarely pure and never simple, even when the effect of such frankness proves disconcerting to the blind optimism of the faithful.

> Shall we conceal the Case, or tell it—
> We who believe the evidence ? [1]

he asks. The result is often the unwelcome story told by the trees of Yell'ham Wood : " Life offers— to deny ! " [2] but this sort of pessimism does not completely drain away from man the joy of braving life with an indomitable spirit, as does the more cynical and bitter lack of faith in human nature that darkened the last years of Mark Twain, and that finds treatment as beautifully ironic as it is unusual, in Hardy's *Ah, Are You Digging on My Grave ?* " (*SC*).

Hardy's basic optimism, paradoxical as that expres-

[1] *The Problem* (*PP*).   [2] *Yell'ham Wood's Story* (*TL*).

sion must sound to his superficial readers and critics, may best be observed in his underlying humanity, in the ground-tone of pity that sounds through all his work no less than it does through the philosophy of Schopenhauer, and in the feeling, in which he is again in harmony with the great philosopher of the Will, that " man's greatest enemy is man ! "

APPENDIX

CHRONOLOGICAL LIST OF HARDY'S WRITINGS [1]

1865. How I Built Myself a House (*Chambers's Journal*).

1871. Desperate Remedies.

1872. Under the Greenwood Tree.

1873. A Pair of Blue Eyes.

1874. Far from the Madding Crowd.

1876. The Hand of Ethelberta.

1878. The Return of the Native.

1879. The Dorsetshire Labourer (*Longman's Magazine*).

1880. The Trumpet-Major.

1881. A Laodicean.

1882. Two on a Tower.

1886. The Mayor of Casterbridge.
  Obituary Essay on William Barnes (*Athenæum*).

1887. The Woodlanders.

1888. Wessex Tales.
  The Profitable Reading of Fiction (*Forum*).

1890. Candour in English Fiction (*New Review*).

1891. The Science of Fiction (*New Review*).
  A Group of Noble Dames.
  Tess of the D'Urbervilles.

---

[1] This list is by no means a complete bibliography ; it includes only works of major importance and interest.

1892. The Well Beloved (*Revised,* 1897).

1894. Life's Little Ironies.

On the Tree of Knowledge (*New Review*).

1895. Jude the Obscure.

1898. Wessex Poems.[1]

1901. Poems of the Past and the Present.[1]

1903. The Dynasts, Part One (dated 1904).

1906. The Dynasts, Part Two.

1908. The Dynasts, Part Three.

1909. Time's Laughingstocks.[1]

1913. A Changed Man, and Other Tales.

1914. Satires of Circumstance.[1]

1917. Moments of Vision.[1]

1922. Late Lyrics and Earlier.[1]

1923. The Famous Tragedy of the Queen of Cornwall.

---

[1] These volumes contain many early poems, some of them written as far back as 1866. Hardy wrote verse continually throughout his career, and has always regarded himself primarily as a poet; but such poems as he offered for publication before his reputation as a novelist had been established were almost invariably returned by editors as unsuitable.

INDEX

Æschylus, 7
  Prometheus, Pers., 107
Angelus Silesius, 55
Anglo-Saxon poetry, 106
Animals, 63 sqq.
Archer, William, Real Conversations, 145-6
Aristotle—
  Poetics, 36
  Metaphysics, 59

Beowulf, 7
Bergson, 71
Berkeley, 21

Christianity, 61 sqq., 81 sqq.

Dictionnaire Philosophique, 14
Diogenes Lærtius, 14

Epicurus, 135

Fichte, 21
First Cause, 57 sqq.
Freedom and Necessity, 88 sqq.

Garwood, Helen, 14, 16, 115
Goethe, 7
  Wahlverwandschaften, 20
Gosse, Edmund, 14

Hardy, Thomas—
  'ΑΓΝΩΣΤΩ, ΘΕΩ, 50, 51
  Ah, Are You Digging on My Grave? 147
  Aquæ Sulis, 81
  At a Hasty Wedding, 125
  The Bedridden Peasant to an Unknowing God, 79

Hardy, Thomas (contd.)—
  Before Knowledge, 79
  Birds at Winter Nightfall, 85
  The Blind Bird, 85
  The Burghers, 125
  By the Earth's Corpse, 79
  The Caged Freed and Home Again, 85
  The Caged Goldfinch, 85
  A Changed Man, 125
  The Church-Builder, 83
  The Conformers, 125
  The Convergence of the Twain, 51
  The Curate's Kindness, 83, 125
  The Darkling Thrush, 86
  Desperate Remedies, 36, 37, 38, 39, 41, 82
  The Dream-Follower, 24
  A Dream-Question, 79
  The Dynasts, 7 sqq.
  The Face at the Casement, 108
  The Famous Tragedy of the Queen of Cornwall, 10
  Far from the Madding Crowd, 41, 42, 45, 84
  Fellow Townsmen, 44
  For Life I Had Never Cared Greatly, 19
  Friends Beyond, 142
  God-Forgotten, 79
  God's Education, 79
  God's Funeral, 78, 79
  The Hand of Ethelberta, 14
  Hap, 35, 51
  He Wonders About Himself, 50, 80
  Her Immortality, 142
  Heredity, 98
  His Immortality, 143
  The House of Silence, 144

Thomas Hardy's Universe

Hardy, Thomas (*contd.*)—
The Husband's View, 126
I Said to Love, 124
An Imaginative Woman, 20
The Impercipient, 78
In Church, 83
Interlopers at the Knap, 44
In Vision I Roamed the Flashing Firmament, 18
Jude the Obscure, 7, 14, 23, 48, 49, 84, 126
Late Lyrics and Earlier, 10
Lines, 138
Long Plighted, 125
The Masked Face, 144
The Mayor of Casterbridge, 44, 45, 46
The Memorial Brass, 126
More Love Lyrics, 124
Nature's Questioning, 79
New Year's Eve, 79
On a Fine Morning, 24
On the Tree of Knowledge, 126
Over the Coffin, 125
A Pair of Blue Eyes, 14, 18, 36, 37, 39, 83, 97
The Pedigree, 97
The Pink Frock, 126, 127
A Plaint to Man, 79
The Problem, 147
The Profitable Reading of Fiction, 22
The Puzzled Game-Birds, 85
The Respectable Burgher on the Higher Criticism, 78
The Return of the Native, 14, 43, 44, 45, 67, 84
The Rival, 126
The Roman Gravemounds, 76
Rose-Ann, 126
Royal Sponsors, 82
The Sleep-Walker, 68
The Subalterns, 68
The Sweet Hussy, 126
The Temporary the All, 97
Tess of the D'Urbervilles, 7, 14, 22, 47, 48, 82, 84, 107, 136
To a Motherless Child, 68
The To-Be-Forgotten, 143
To Outer Nature, 68

Hardy, Thomas (*contd.*)—
The Torn Letter, 108
A Trampwoman's Tragedy, 126
Transformations, 144
The Trumpet-Major, 41
Two on a Tower, 43, 48, 82
Under the Greenwood Tree, 37
The Voice of Things, 68
Wagtail and Baby, 86
The Well-Beloved, 14, 23
A Wife and Another, 125
The Withered Arm, 19
The Woman in the Rye, 108
The Woodlanders, 14, 21, 46, 47
The Wound, 68
Yell'ham Wood's Story, 147
Hedgcock, F. A., 14, 16
Hegel, 21
Hindu philosophy, 16, 64
Humboldt, 14

Judaism, 60, 61, 81

Kant, 17, 21, 24
Koran, 61

Leibnitz, 25
Leopardi, 7, 47

Maeterlinck, 139, 140
Mark Twain, 147
Materialism, 64, *sqq.*
Monism, 66, 77

Nature, 42 *sqq.*, 47, 49
Nemesis, 7, 47, 49
Nietzsche, 31
    Also Sprach Zarathustra, 79

Peripatetic School, 14
Pessimism, 15, 129 *sqq.*
Pindar, 107
Plato, 14, 21
Preacher, 131

Religion, 60 *sqq.*

Schiller, 56
Schleiermacher, 14
Scholastic Philosophers, 25, 90

Index

Schopenhauer, Arthur—
  Die beiden Grundprobleme der Ethik, 89
  Freiheit des Willens, 91
  Das Fundament der Moral, 134
  Geschichte der Lehre vom Idealen und Realen, 18
  Metaphysik der Geschlechtsliebe, 113
  Parerga und Paralipomena, 18, 62, 89
  Ueber Religion, 62
  Vergleichende, Anatomie, 27
  Versuch ueber Geistersehen, 105
  Vierfache Wurzel, 25
  Vom Instinkt und Kunsttrieb, 27

Schopenhauer, Arthur (*contd.*)—
  Vom Primat des Willens in Selbstbewusstsein, 111
  Die Welt als Wille und Vorstellung, 15 *sqq.*
  Der Wille in der Natur, 27

Shelley, 7, 23
Socrates, 14
Spinoza, 9, 14, 21
Swinburne, *Hymn to Proserpina*, 81

Utilitarianism, 14

Voltaire, 7

Wilde, Oscar, 147
Wyrd, 7, 38